Thwarting Death

Matthew J. Greife

Thwarting Death

A Legal Culture of Resistance Among Colorado Death Penalty Defense Lawyers

Matthew J. Greife
Social and Cultural Sciences
Marquette University
Milwaukee, WI, USA

ISBN 978-3-031-46132-3   ISBN 978-3-031-46133-0 (eBook)
https://doi.org/10.1007/978-3-031-46133-0

© The Editor(s) (if applicable) and The Author(s), under exclusive license to Springer Nature Switzerland AG 2023

This work is subject to copyright. All rights are solely and exclusively licensed by the Publisher, whether the whole or part of the material is concerned, specifically the rights of translation, reprinting, reuse of illustrations, recitation, broadcasting, reproduction on microfilms or in any other physical way, and transmission or information storage and retrieval, electronic adaptation, computer software, or by similar or dissimilar methodology now known or hereafter developed.
The use of general descriptive names, registered names, trademarks, service marks, etc. in this publication does not imply, even in the absence of a specific statement, that such names are exempt from the relevant protective laws and regulations and therefore free for general use.
The publisher, the authors, and the editors are safe to assume that the advice and information in this book are believed to be true and accurate at the date of publication. Neither the publisher nor the authors or the editors give a warranty, expressed or implied, with respect to the material contained herein or for any errors or omissions that may have been made. The publisher remains neutral with regard to jurisdictional claims in published maps and institutional affiliations.

This Palgrave Macmillan imprint is published by the registered company Springer Nature Switzerland AG
The registered company address is: Gewerbestrasse 11, 6330 Cham, Switzerland

"Government is not reason, it is not eloquence, it is force…Never for a moment should it be left to irresponsible action."

—*George Washington*

Acknowledgments

There are so many people to thank. First and foremost—thank you to everyone who participated in this study. I cannot use your names but please know that I'm forever grateful for your time, insights, commitment to the practice of criminal defense and how you influenced me personally to fight tooth and nail for my clients being prosecuted, or as I said in court more than once, persecuted by the government. To Mark Pogrebin—thank you so much for wanting me to be involved with this project and for all your guidance after passing the torch. I never would have begun this project if you had not initially pitched it and wanted to work on this together. Finally, to all my friends and family who have supported me throughout the years with your love and encouragement.

Contents

1	**Introduction**	1
	A Legal Culture of Resistance	10
	Why Study Death Penalty Defense Lawyer Culture?	14
	Why Study Colorado Death Penalty Defense Lawyers?	18
	Participants, Methods and Layout of This Book	21
2	**Seeds of Resistance: Skepticism and Questioning of the Government**	25
	Pre-College Years	27
	The College Years	31
	Outliers	33
	Conclusion	35
3	**The Socializing Experiences of Law School & Internships**	37
	Internships for the Criminal Defense Minded	39
	Internships for Those Finding Their Way	42
	Interning with the Prosecutors Then the Defense	48
	Conclusion	50

4 **Empathy & Moral Anger: The Emotional Components of a Legal Culture of Resistance** 53
   Empathy in Death Penalty Defense Work 55
   Empathy and the Client 58
   Empathy, Victim's Families and Society 64
      Moral Anger Towards the Death Penalty 66
   Conclusion 70

5 **Active Resistance—Creating Ideological Boundaries and the Fight Within** 73
   Judges 74
   Prosecutors 85
   Adequacy of Resources 96
   Aggressive Litigation Strategies: An Overview 101
   Mitigation 105
   Litigation 108
   Conclusion 118

6 **Sacrifice Within a Culture of Resistance** 121
   Conclusion 129

7 **Conclusion** 131

Epilog 139

About the Author

Matthew Greife is currently an assistant teaching professor at Marquette University in Milwaukee, WI. Prior to entering academia, Matthew worked as a criminal defense and civil rights attorney for Baumgartner Law, LLC and eventually was promoted to director of civil rights litigation. Over the years, Matthew won numerous acquittals in criminal defense cases and secured significant financial settlements for those who were wrongfully abused and arrested by law enforcement officials. Now, Matthew researches topics and teaches courses on corrections, law and society and environmental criminology. He enjoys spending time fishing, cheering on the Green Bay Packers, remaining a thumb in the eye to America's criminal processing system and playing with his dog Leia who is the "heart of the rebellion."

1

Introduction

This is an ethnographic monograph about death penalty defense lawyers in Colorado. My primary goal with this monograph is simple and straight forward: to show that Colorado death penalty defense lawyers practice law within a 'legal culture of resistance.' Later in this introduction, I will explain in detail the concept of a legal culture of resistance and why this monograph narrowly focuses on Colorado death penalty defense lawyers. For now, I want to focus more on the personal stories, beliefs and perspectives of some of the best criminal defense attorneys in the United States that this book relies upon. The salience in telling these personal stories is more than academic—it is a demonstration that legal processes are interwoven with broader social and cultural narratives. Each individual attorney, through their efforts in trying to stop their clients from being executed by the government, became interwoven within the larger discussion over capital punishment. On one hand, by defending people facing the death penalty and trying to save their lives, these lawyers legitimized formal legal processes governing the implementation of capital punishment because every time a person was spared from the gallows people could point to the successes and say "the system works."

On the other hand, each time the death penalty defense lawyers successfully thwarted the government's attempt to secure an execution, the body politic was free to ask a simple question: "do we need or want the death penalty?" The work of Colorado death penalty defense lawyers created a space where the necessity of capital punishment was being discussed so it is important to know who these individuals are and how their backgrounds influenced litigation styles that would influence social change. As such, before getting to the more traditional academic components of a monograph, I want to begin at the ending of Colorado's story with the death penalty—the social change stemming from the work of the individual attorneys—abolition of capital punishment.

On March 23, 2020, Colorado became the 22nd state to prohibit the death penalty since the *Gregg v. Georgia*[1] decision in 1976 reinstating the death penalty after capital punishment was determined to be cruel and unusual and thereby a violation of the Constitution's 8th amendment.[2] Unlike Washington State which saw its death penalty abolished through judicial proclamation, calling it unconstitutional because it was imposed arbitrarily and in a racially biased manner,[3] Colorado's ban on capital punishment came through legislative decree.[4]

Prohibition of capital punishment in Colorado, unlike Washington State,[5] did not mean prosecutors must stop pursuing the two active death penalty cases against Dreion Dearing and Marco Garcia-Bravo that were still pending as of March 23, 2020. Nor did abolishing the death penalty mean that Nathan Dunlap, Sir Mario Owens and Robert Ray[6]—the three men on death row at the time of abolition—could not be executed. Therefore, on the same day, he signed the legislation abolishing the death penalty, Colorado's governor Jared Polis commuted Dunlap's, Owens'

---

[1] 428 U.S. 153 (1976).
[2] *Furman v. Georgia*, 408 U.S. 238 (1972).
[3] *State v. Gregory*, 427 P.3d 621 (Wash. 2018).
[4] Senate Bill 20-100.
[5] After the *Gregory* decision was delivered on October 11, 2018, all death sentences were immediately converted to a term of life in prison and pending capital cases were no longer eligible to ask for the death penalty.
[6] Sir Mario Owens and Robert Ray were given a death sentence for their roles in the murder of Javad Fields and his fiancé Vivian Wolfe. Javad Fields was the son of state Senator Rhonda Fields—a democrat from Aurora that is strongly against repealing the death penalty.

and Ray's death sentences to life without the possibility of parole. All that remained were the two pending death penalty cases. Dearing's trial had not yet begun and Garcia-Bravo was set to begin his second trial because the first prosecution ended in a hung jury on the murder charges.[7]

As a result of abolition and the commutations of Dunlap, Owens and Ray's death sentences, Dave Young, the elected district attorney in Colorado's 17th judicial district, announced on March 30, 2020, that his office will stop pursuing the death penalty against Dreion Dearing for the murder of an Adams County Sheriff's Deputy because he feared even if they secured a death sentence, Governor Polis would just commute it to life without the possibility of parole.[8] About two weeks after Dave Young's announcement Dan May, the elected district attorney in Colorado's 4th judicial district dropped the death penalty against Marco Garcia-Bravo for the murder of two high school students. May echoed the statements from Dave Young and said that Governor Polis has made himself a '13th juror' and would likely block a death sentence with the stroke of a pen.[9] Such claims about Governor Polis possibly commuting the death sentences of Dearing and Garcia-Bravo (assuming juries gave a death sentence—nobody has been sentenced to die in Colorado since 2009) are likely right because Polis stated "*…the commutations of these despicable and guilty individuals [Dunlap, Owens and Ray] are consistent with the abolition of the death penalty in the State of Colorado, and consistent with the recognition that the death penalty cannot be, and never has been, administered equitably in the State of Colorado.*[10]" Thus, as of April 13, 2020, the death penalty in Colorado was abolished.

---

[7] Grewe, Lyndsey (2021). New Trial Date Set for Final Suspect in Double-Murder of Coronado Teens. February 11, 2021. https://www.kktv.com/2021/02/11/new-trial-date-set-for-final-suspect-in-double-murder-of-coronado-teens/.

[8] Death Penalty Information Center (2020). Colorado District Attorneys Drop One Capital Prosecution, Continue a Second, After State Abolishes Death Penalty. https://deathpenaltyinfo.org/news/colorado-district-attorneys-drop-one-capital-prosecution-continue-a-second-after-state-abolishes-death-penalty. April 1, 2020.

[9] Death Penalty Information Center (2020). News Brief—Prosecutors Drop Death Penalty in Last Remaining Colorado Capital Prosecution. April 13, 2020. https://deathpenaltyinfo.org/stories/news-brief-prosecutors-drop-death-penalty-in-last-remaining-colorado-capital-prosecution.

[10] Keeney, Andrew (2020). Colorado Death Penalty Abolished, Polis Commutes Sentences of Death Row Inmates. March 23, 2020. https://www.cpr.org/2020/03/23/polis-signs-death-penalty-repeal-commutes-sentences-of-death-row-inmates/.

That said, the abolition of Colorado's death penalty was never really a question of 'if' but 'when.' As the sociologist and a leading expert about the death penalty in Colorado Professor Michael Radelet stated "Coloradans have always been ambivalent about the death penalty" despite polling showing citizens are, depending on the poll, in favor of capital punishment as a possible punishment.[11] This history of ambivalence towards capital punishment in Colorado underpins why full and public discussions about the efficacy and necessity of the death penalty were brought to the social and political forefront after life sentences were granted to James Eagan Holmes and Dexter Lewis.[12]

The citizens of Colorado, and frankly the country, were shaken when news broke that on July 20, 2012, James Holmes killed 13 people and wounded 70 others when he opened fire with an AR-15 into a crowded movie theater playing the midnight showing of 'The Dark Knight.' For the next three years, victims and their families, citizens, commentators and talking heads would intensely watch and analyze the trial of James Holmes and wonder if prosecutors would succeed in securing a death sentence and send him to 'death row.' On August 7, 2015, James Holmes was sentenced to life in prison without the possibility of parole ("LWOP") instead of death. Barely three weeks later, Dexter Lewis who, along with other individuals stabbed five people to death during a robbery that netted around $170, was given LWOP over a death sentence. These two life sentences were a clear sign that there are enough Coloradans who are 'death qualified[13]' but nevertheless reluctant

---

[11] Radelet, Michael L. (2017: 166). *The History of the Death Penalty in Colorado*. University Press of Colorado: Boulder, CO.

[12] I went onto the Denver Post's website (www.denverpost.com) and just did a general search for the "Death Penalty" and found multiple links for citizen and political commentary on the death penalty arguing for and against the punishment. The following are just a couple links to the public debates that took place in the Denver Post: https://www.denverpost.com/2015/09/05/the-death-penalty-and-two-colorado-murder-trials-5-letters/; https://www.denverpost.com/2019/02/01/colorado-death-penalty-repeal/; https://www.denverpost.com/2015/06/13/debating-the-death-penalty-3-letters/.

[13] In essence, to serve on a jury where the death penalty could be invoked jurors must not (a) be completely unwilling to ever impose a sentence of death or (b) completely unwilling to consider a life sentence without the possibility of parole (LWOP). See generally: *Witherspoon v. Illinois*, 391 U.S. 510 (1968); *Lockhart v. McCree*, 476 U.S. 162 (1986).

to approve the execution of another person no matter how horrific the crimes.

In Colorado, it is required by law that a jury decide if a person is to be executed or not and the decision for death must be unanimous.[14] Based on the law, if only one juror decides against the death penalty, then a judge is mandated to impose a life sentence. Almost immediately after the Holmes and Lewis life sentences, George Brauchler, the elected district attorney in Colorado's 18th Judicial District who prosecuted the Holmes case, went to the papers and claimed that the death penalty was only avoided for James Holmes because of a single 'hold out' juror[15] when in reality, three of the twelve jurors decided death was not the appropriate sentence.[16] Brauchler's goal was clear—keep the death penalty in place despite the two surprising life sentences for Holmes and Lewis.

During the four years after Holmes' and Lewis' life sentences, pro-death penalty advocates would publicly make statements and write op-eds in favor of keeping the death penalty as a viable option in punishment and sentencing.[17] However, these efforts were met by more and more voices publicly demanding a repeal of the death penalty. The calls for abolition after the Holmes and Lewis life verdicts argued that capital punishment in Colorado appeared to be for all intent and purpose obsolete[18] because, in regard to the death penalty, "juries themselves wanted no part of it.[19]" As such, the Colorado legislature could base its political

---

[14] C.R.S. 18-1.3-1201(2)(d).

[15] Nelson, Kristen, Tamara Brady and Daniel King (2016: 612–614). "The Evil Defendant and the Holdout Juror: Unpacking the Myths of the Aurora Theater Shooting Case as we Ponder the Future of Capital Punishment in Colorado." *Denver Law Review*, 93(3): 595–634.

[16] Id.

[17] Brauchler, George (2019). Coloradans Should Have the Final Say on the Death Penalty (and I'd Hope They Keep It). https://www.denverpost.com/2019/03/01/brauchler-coloradans-should-have-the-final-say-on-the-death-penalty-and-id-hope-they-keep-it/.

[18] Sentinel Editorial Board (2019). Proponents of Colorado's Death Penalty Make Convincing Arguments to Repeal It Now—Do It. https://sentinelcolorado.com/opinion/editorial-proponents-of-colorados-death-penalty-make-convincing-arguments-to-repeal-it-now-do-it/; The Denver Post (2015). A Looming Crisis for Death Penalty. https://www.denverpost.com/2015/08/11/a-looming-crisis-for-death-penalty/.

[19] The Denver Post (2015). Dexter Lewis Verdict Sends a Message on Colorado's death penalty. https://www.denverpost.com/2015/08/27/dexter-lewis-verdict-sends-a-message-on-colorados-death-penalty.

decision to repeal the death penalty on a social consensus for abolition which eventually happened.

Ultimately, Colorado's repealing of the death penalty was a political decision but it is not one that occurred in a political vacuum. Sociologist David Garland argues that "...crime control and criminal justice [is] affected by changes in the social organization of the societies in which it functions....[20]" Garland also argues that a primary reason the death penalty remains a method of punishment is that it is essentially a 'communication system':

> It [the death penalty] is about mounting campaigns, talking polls, passing laws, bringing charges, bargaining pleas, imposing sentences and rehearing cases. It is about threats rather than deeds, anticipated deaths rather than actual executions. What gets performed, for the most part, is discourse and debate.[21]

Garland's point is demonstrated by the actions of George Brauchler after the Holmes and Lewis life sentences. In one of his many op-eds, Brauchler argued that the death penalty is 'justice' in the retributive sense as illustrated by this specific quote: "*...for the worst of the worst murderers justice is death...the repeal of the death penalty treats all murders as the same. Once a person commits a single act of murder, each additional murder is a freebie. That is not justice.*[22]" Shortly after writing his op-ed, Brauchler publicly announced he was considering pursuing the death penalty in two different cases but after receiving some public criticism[23] declined to pursue capital charges. Finally, just before being term limited out of his role as elected district attorney and, on the heels of failed gubernatorial and attorney general campaigns, Brauchler decided

---

[20] Garland, David (2001: 193). *The Culture of Control: Crime and Social Order in Contemporary Society*. University of Chicago Press: Chicago, IL.
[21] Garland, David (2010: 312). *Peculiar Institution: America's Death Penalty in an Age of Abolition*. Harvard University Press: Cambridge, MA.
[22] Supra Footnote 17.
[23] Ehrlich, Peter (2016). The Insanity of Once Again Considering the Death Penalty in Colorado. https://www.denverpost.com/2016/09/28/the-insanity-of-once-again-considering-the-death-penalty-in-colorado/; Cherner, Phil (2016). Political Motivation for DA Brauchler in Seeking the Death Penalty? https://www.denverpost.com/2016/12/09/political-motivation-for-da-brauchler-seeking-death-penalty/.

without explanation to not pursue the death penalty against Devon Erickson who killed Kendrick Castillo during a mass shooting at a STEM school in Highlands Ranch, CO[24] despite initial public statements to the contrary.

For all the public discourse from George Brauchler and other pro-capital punishment prosecutors such as district attorney Jim Bullock, their voices represented what appears to be a very loud minority of people in Colorado. Colorado Attorney General Phil Weiser and well-known prosecutors such as Beth McCann from Denver and Michael Dougherty from Boulder were very public in making it known they wanted capital punishment to be abolished.[25] State Senator Rhonda Fields, whose son was murdered by death row inmates Sir Mario Owens and Robert Ray, was one of the few democrats in Colorado to publicly support capital punishment but her voice was drowned out by democratic colleagues and a number of popular republicans such as State Senator Kevin Priola.[26]

A hallmark of American punishment is that the public, through popular opinion, is capable of influencing penal policy.[27] Capital punishment is, as argued by David Garland, very much a function of state and local punitive preferences.[28] This makes sense because in contemporary America, less than 1% of the nation's local counties sentence people to death which is in stark contrast to the frequent use of capital punishment during the 1980s and 90s.[29] The same national trends exist in Colorado where of all possible first-degree murders that could result in the death penalty only 3% are actually charged as a capital offense, 1%

---

[24] Associated Press (2020). Prosecutors Won't Seek Death Penalty Against Older of Two Suspected STEM School Highlands Ranch Shooters. https://coloradosun.com/2020/03/06/devon-erickson-stem-school-highlands-ranch-death-penalty/.

[25] Paul, Jesse (2019). Colorado Lawmakers Will Consider Whether to Repeal the Death Penalty Again, as Factors Align for Passage. https://coloradosun.com/2019/03/03/colorado-death-penalty-repeal-effort/.

[26] Id.

[27] See generally: Zimring, Franklin E., Gordon Hawkins and Sam Kamin (2001). *Punishment and Democracy: Three Strikes and You're Out in California*. Oxford University Press: New York.

[28] Supra Footnote 21 at p. 26.

[29] Garrett, Brandon L., Alexander Jakubow and Ankur Desaiy (2017). "The American Death Penalty in Decline." *The Journal of Criminal Law & Criminology*, 107(4): 561–642; Phillips, Scott and Trent Steidley (2020). "A Systematic Lottery: The Texas Death Penalty, 1976 to 2016." *Columbia Human Rights Review*, 51(3): 1041–1069.

of these cases make it to sentencing and 0.6% end in a death sentence.[30] These trends matter. As Daniel LaChance argues inevitably, the retributive rhetoric employed by death penalty supporters will lead to a cultural disillusion with the death penalty because it will become publicly known that capital punishment fails to live up to its retributive promise.[31]

Ironically then, capital punishments biggest supporters may have been a significant cause of its demise because Coloradans saw through public debate that (1) the death penalty is used very sparingly as a possible method of punishment as acknowledged by capital punishment supporter district attorney Jim Bullock,[32] and (2) even when used for the "most horrific murders," defendants are not being given a death sentence by jurors. Thus, public debate kept open this very important social and political question: "if the death penalty is hardly ever used and nobody is going to death row why do we have it?" The Colorado legislature answered that question on March 23, 2020, when it abolished capital punishment.

Colorado's debate over capital punishment would not have remained so prominent without the Herculean efforts of death penalty defense attorneys. To be fair, there are a number of outside organizations that advocated for the abolition of capital punishment such as the Coloradans for Alternatives to the Death Penalty ("CADP") and many others that helped influence public debates on capital punishment. However, in the end, it was the death penalty defense lawyers that needed to take these cases on and win LWOP sentences. Since capital punishment had been reinstated after the *Gregg*[33] decision, Colorado prosecutors have brought numerous death penalty cases that more often than not end with defendants receiving life sentences. The James Holmes case is probably the most famous life sentence secured by Colorado death penalty defense lawyers but there are numerous others. For example, Jim Bullock as district attorney in the 16th District sought the death penalty (against

---

[30] Marceau, Justin, Sam Kamin and Wanda Foglia (2013). "Death Eligibility in Colorado: Many Are Called, Few Are Chosen." *The University of Denver Law Review*, 84: 1070–1115.

[31] LaChance, Daniel (2016: 185). *Executing Freedom: The Cultural Life of Capital Punishment in the United States*. The University of Chicago Press: Chicago, IL.

[32] Supra Footnote 25.

[33] Supra Footnote 1.

the wishes of the victim's family) for Miguel Contreras-Perez's murder of correctional officer Mary Ricard; after spending over $1.6 million dollars, the prosecution ended in a life sentence.[34] Dan May as the District Attorney for the 4th district saw a jury give Glen Lew Galloway a life sentence for the murder of his ex-girlfriend and a witness to the homicide.[35] As a final example, Edward Herrera received four life sentences after pleading guilty to binding four people with duct tape and shooting them in the head while the 3 year old daughter of one of the victims witnessed the killings.[36]

With every life sentence secured by Colorado death penalty defense attorneys for what can only be described as horrific and tragic murders, the public discourse discussed above would begin anew and continue until the next life sentence. Prosecutors and politicians supporting the death penalty were constantly trying to explain that despite constant failures in securing a death sentence, capital punishment is a necessity because it is a deterrent and retributive justice. In the end, the death penalty in Colorado was revealed to be 'merely performative' as argued by Garland and unable to live up to its retributive ideals as argued by LaChance which served as solid social and political foundations for abolition.

Nevertheless, for all their importance, very little is known about death penalty defense lawyers personally or culturally. Capital defense is among the most complex fields of litigation in all of law and requires defense lawyers be more than just attorneys—they become confidants, advisors and therapists[37] to their client. Moreover, the best death penalty defense

---

[34] Death Penalty Information Center (2019). Colorado Taxpayers Paid DA's Office $1.6 Million for Unsuccessfully Pursuing Death Penalty Against Wishes of Victim's Family. https://deathpenaltyinfo.org/news/colorado-taxpayers-paid-das-office-1-6-million-for-unsuccessfully-pursuing-death-penalty-against-wishes-of-victims-family.

[35] Benzel, Lance (2018). No Death Penalty for Galloway Jury Decides. https://gazette.com/news/no-death-penalty-for-double-killer-galloway-jury-decides/article_32d4c3dc-7eea-11e8-93b7-9b905eebf163.html.

[36] Supra Footnote 11: Radelet (2017: 170). Phillips, Noelle (2015). Victim in Notorious 2003 Denver Murder Case Dies from Wounds 11 Years Later. https://www.denverpost.com/2015/05/14/victim-in-notorious-2003-denver-murder-case-dies-from-wounds-11-years-later/.

[37] Goodrum, Sarah, Mark Pogrebin and Matthew J. Greife (2015). "Representing the Underdog: The Righteous Development of Death Penalty Defense Attorneys." *Criminal Law Bulletin*, 51(2): 329–357.

lawyers invest their heart and soul into sparing clients from execution by engaging in long, uphill legal battles that are emotionally and physically exhausting.[38] Studying death penalty lawyers does more than help us understand the legal culture these attorneys create and perpetuate—it helps us understand how law and social attitudes can be shaped one case at a time.

A Legal Culture of Resistance

There is a myriad of ways scholars have utilized the concept of legal culture. In its most basic sense, legal culture provides a framework to broadly identify cultural categories and facts about local institutions such as the role of attorneys in the courtroom, decisions about when to engage law and even values, mindsets and ideals of legal actors.[39] David Nelkin put it succinctly when he said: "Like culture itself, legal culture is about who we are not just what we do.[40]" As such, legal culture, whether it be the study of norms, values, mindsets, socialization processes, outcomes or conditions upon which law is engaged, can be studied at different levels ranging from the globalized world,[41] nation states[42] and all the way down to a specific city or courtroom.[43]

---

[38] Kaplan, Paul (2010). "Forgetting the Future: Cause Lawyering and the Work of California Capital Trial Defenders." *Theoretical Criminology*, 14(2): 211–235; Sheffer, Suzanna (2013). *Fighting for Their Lives: Inside the Experience of Capital Defense Attorneys*. Vanderbilt University: Nashville, TN.

[39] Nelken, David (2004). Using the Concept of Legal Culture. https://escholarship.org/uc/item/7dk1j7hm.

[40] Id.

[41] Engel, David and Jaruwan S. Engel (2010). *Tort, Custom and Karma: Globalization and Legal Consciousness in Thailand*. Stanford University Press: Stanford, CA.

[42] Feldman, Eric A. (2000). Blood Justice: Courts, Conflict and Compensation in Japan, France and the United States. *Law & Society Review*, 34(3): 651–701.

[43] Church, Thomas W. (1985). "Examining Local Legal Culture." *American Bar Foundation Research Journal*, Summer Issue: 449–518; Harris, John C. and Paul Jesilow (2000). "It's Not the Old Ball Game: Three Strikes and the Courtroom Workgroup." *Justice Quarterly*, 17(1): 185–203; Metcalfe, Christi (2016). "The Role of Courtroom Workgroups in Felony Case Dispositions: An Analysis of Workgroup Familiarity and Similarity." *Law & Society Review*, 50(3): 637–673; Rudes, Danielle S. and Shannon Portillo (2012). "Roles and Power within Federal Problem Solving Courtroom Workgroups." *Law & Policy*, 34(4): 402–427.

To be fair, because the concept of legal culture is incredibly broad and encompasses a massive amount of social phenomena, it can be difficult to operationalize. Lawrence Friedman, the professor who popularized the idea of legal culture, states that as an abstraction legal culture is 'slippery' and rife with problems about concrete definitions.[44] However, muddled the concept of legal culture, it is still utilized in various forms.[45] For instance, Professor Friedman created distinctions he refers to as internal and external legal culture.[46] External legal culture is the makeup of opinions, interests and influences weighing upon the law that is mobilized by various social organizations.[47] Internal legal culture refers to the practices, behaviors and understandings of legal professionals.[48] Others have created the concept of 'local legal cultures'[49] to serve as a workable construct. Nevertheless, the critique of legal culture remains that despite being an interesting concept, it still lacks an explanatory component.[50] As such, scholars such as Susan Silbey argue that due to an overall vagueness of the legal culture concept, it should be used in conjuncture with other explanatory frameworks such as legal consciousness.[51]

I tend to agree with Silbey that the concept of legal culture should be used in conjuncture with other frameworks and theoretical premises.

---

[44] Friedman, Lawrence (2006). "The Place of Legal Culture in the Sociology of Law." In: Michael Freeman (ed) *Law and Sociology*, 185–199. Oxford University Press.

[45] See generally: Engel-Merry, Sally (2010). "What Is Legal Culture? An Anthropological Perspective." *The Journal of Comparative Law*, 1(1): 40–58; Montana, Riccardo (2012). "Adversarialism in Italy: Using the Concept of Legal Culture to Understand Resistance to Legal Modifications and Its Consequences." *European Journal of Crime, Criminal Law and Criminal Justice* (20): 99–120.

[46] Supra Footnote 47. See also: Friedman, Lawrence M. (1975). *The Legal System: A Social Science Perspective*. The Russell Sage Foundation: New York; Friedman, Lawrence M. (2006). "The Place of Legal Culture in the Society of Law." In: Michael Freeman (ed) *Law and Sociology: Current Legal Issues Volume 8*. Oxford University Press: New York.

[47] Id.

[48] Id.

[49] See: Kritzer, Herbert M. and Frances K. Zemans (1993). "Local Legal Culture and the Control of Litigation." *Law and Society Review*, 27(3): 535–558; Sullivan, Teresa A., Elizabeth Warren and Jay Lawrence Westbrook (1994). The Persistence of Local Legal Culture: Twenty Years of Evidence from the Federal Bankruptcy Courts. *Harvard Journal of Law and Public Policy*, 17(3): 801–836.

[50] Supra Footnote 43 at 41.

[51] Silbey, Susan (2001). "Legal Culture and Legal Consciousness." In: *International Encyclopedia of Social and Behavioral Sciences*. Pergamon Press: New York, at 8624.

For this monograph, I utilize Professor Henry Giroux's 'a culture of resistance[52]' in conjuncture with the broader concept of legal culture to discover the meaning of each participant's backgrounds and manifest behaviors. Giroux's culture of resistance was written in regard to the field of education but it has been extended, albeit in very limited instances, into other social contexts[53] making it a versatile analytical tool. In Giroux's framework, 'culture' and 'resistance' are two different concepts that can be brought together for analytical and explanatory purposes.

For Giroux, culture is in the broadest sense a product of relational interactions occurring between classes/groups bounded together through various social, political and economic forces and informed by a wide range of experiences mediated by the exercise of power by dominant groups.[54] A key point here is that culture is "constituted as a dialectical instance of power and conflict, rooted in the struggle over both material conditions and the form and content of practical activity[55]" which is informed by larger dynamics of history.[56] As such, cultures, whether they be embodied by the norms, values and mores of a dominant or subordinate group, are never pre-determined or static, can repress social groups or transform an existing social order.[57]

Analytically, culture is a 'critical construct' when used to investigate the concrete behaviors that characterize the multitude of relational interactions occurring between dominant and subordinate groups over time and place.[58] Ideology, interpretations of lived experiences, interests of dominant classes, institutional beliefs and practices are all forces

---

[52] Giroux, Henry A. (2001). *Theory and Resistance in Education: Towards a Pedagogy for the Opposition, 2nd Ed*. Bergin & Garvey: Westport, CT.

[53] For example, the concept is used to be a general descriptor of political behavior. "Culture of resistance is one which public challenges to the abuse of power by a regime becomes a norm for activists and a visible segment of the general public" [Press, Robert (2015). "Establishing a Culture of Resistance." In: Robert M. Press (ed) *Ripples of Hope: How Ordinary People Resist Repression Without Violence*. Amsterdam University Press.

[54] Id. at 163.

[55] Id.

[56] Id. at 164.

[57] Id.

[58] Id.

that can act as cultural forces of oppression, resistance or even indifference[59]—this list is by no means exhaustive. The goal for researchers is to determine where in social time and space—a cultural arena if you will—different cultures interact through the various, identifiable forces previously listed, and work to reproduce (i.e., a hegemonic state) or transform the current social and cultural order.

Resistance as a concept asks researchers to see the affirmative act[s] of resisting as "mode[s] of discourse that rejects traditional explanations"[60] about the existence and persistence of social phenomena. Specifically, resistance for Giroux is primarily related to a logic of *moral and political indignation* held by a person or social grouping.[61] Theoretically speaking, Giroux's construct of resistance is based upon three primary assumptions. First, resistance "celebrates a dialectical notion of human agency that rightly portrays domination as neither a static process nor one that is ever complete.[62]" Second, the exercise of power is never one-dimensional (i.e., only expressed by a dominant group).[63] Third, acts of resistance at some level, is an expression of hope for major and radical social changes.[64] As such, analyzing acts of resistance should be an attempt to reveal the implicit or explicit reasons to fight against forces engaging in domination and submission.[65] In order to analyze acts of resistance, then it is incumbent upon researchers to (a) analyze the behavior interpretations as provided by research subjects or (b) investigate the specific historical and relational conditions from which the resistant behaviors develop.[66] My goal in this monograph is to do both.

---

[59] Id. See also: O'Hearn, Denis (2009: 492). "Repression and Solidary Cultures of Resistance: Irish Political Prisoners on Protest." *American Journal of Sociology*, 115(2): 491–526.

[60] Giroux (2001) at 107. Here, Giroux was discussing how the concept of resistance is a mode of discourse that rejects *traditional explanations of school failure and oppositional behavior.*

[61] Id.

[62] Id. at 108.

[63] Id.

[64] Id.

[65] Id. at 109.

[66] Id.

Why Study Death Penalty Defense Lawyer Culture?

Overall scholars have not dedicated much effort to understanding the culture of death penalty defense lawyers. There are two books, one by Susannah Sheffer[67] and the other by Jon Gould & Mary Pagni Barack[68] that take a focused look at the lived experiences, motivations and emotional challenges of capital defense lawyers actively engaged in death penalty defense work. Both books are fantastic and provide a very rich and compelling narrative of the lived experiences death penalty defense lawyers working all across the United States have while practicing. However, neither book seems to describe nor elucidate the culture created by the death penalty attorneys interviewed.

Sheffer's book looks specifically at appellate capital defense attorneys working in multiple states and has had a client executed at some point in their career. Appellate attorneys are unique because their advocacy begins after a jury has decided a defendant will be put to death. Sheffer wonderfully details the emotional components of capital appellate work through her descriptions about how the responsibility of trying to save a life weigh on an attorney, the feelings of winning issues on appeal and the motivations and emotional impact of doing the work. As Sheffer puts it her book is an "…exploration of capital defenders' emotional experience…".[69]

One of Sheffer's interviewees named Paul provides the following narrative:

> I began to feel like the prosecutors and courts would do anything they could-not whether they were bound by any truth, but just anything they could think of to assure that people were executed. I'd certainly understood the zeal that prosecutors had, before that. I'd been involved with a number of cases and had won some and lost others and certainly had

---

[67] Sheffer, Susannah (2013). *Fighting For Their Lives: Inside the Experience of Capital Defense Attorneys*. Vanderbilt University Press: Nashville, TN.
[68] Gould, Jon B. and Maya Pagni Barak (2019). *Capital Defense: Inside the Lives of America's Death Penalty Lawyers*. New York University Press: New York.
[69] Supra Footnote 67 at 7.

seen them fight hard, but this seemed to me to be different. It was, no matter what you do, we're going to get you. I was not only angry, but I felt more helpless than I'd ever felt before.[70]

In another interview with a defender named Simon, the following narrative is provided:

> It usually doesn't matter how good you are or how well you do in a case. No matter how hard you work, for the most part you lose. No matter how well-crafted your pleadings, you lose. No matter how correct your arguments are, courts either change the rules or just ignore them and no one holds them accountable. You can file the most brilliant pleadings based on thousands of human hours of effort and get denied, or you can file a one-issue piece of crap and get denied. It's usually the same result in front of most of the courts in the death belt. This phenomena makes this work very difficult for high-achieving, smart, talented attorneys. Big law firm lawyers whom we get to do these cases sometimes really struggle with this. We all do, of course, but I guess those of us in it for good have either just gotten used to it, or gotten real cynical, or internalized the losses, or all of the above.[71]

The narratives Sheffer provides are far more than just emotionally gripping and moving—they give insight into how the capital punishment machine operates. However, Sheffer does not make a concentrated effort to organize the interviews in a way that systematically highlights specific cultural norms and practices of death penalty defense lawyers. None of this is to take away from the work Sheffer did because it is fantastic. My only point here is to say that my work here is different because I attempt to situate the lived experiences of death penalty defense lawyers within a cultural framework that carries with it theoretical and practical implications.

Gould & Barack's book focuses on death penalty defense trial attorneys working throughout the United States—many of whom had a

---

[70] Id. at 71.
[71] Id. at 79.

client executed. Similar to Shaffer's work, Gould & Barack are interested in studying the capital litigation processes effects on the people participating within the system.[72] For instance, in one interview, an attorney named Joan discusses her views on judges and says, "*I haven't met many judges I respect. I respect the office. On the whole, I would rather have a smart mean judge than a stupid mean judge. But most have been stupid and mean.*[73]" Joan's sentiments are similar to other participants in Gould & Barack's book and there are significant similarities death penalty defense lawyers express in their viewpoints on prosecutors and the criminal processing system as a whole.[74] Early on in their book, Gould & Barack argue that death penalty defense lawyers are a unique and distinct community and culture within the field of criminal defense attorneys.[75] I certainly agree with the statement that defense penalty defense lawyers are part of a unique community and culture but Gould & Barack's study is very similar to Shaffer's work in that, the lived experiences, perspectives and effects capital litigation have on the defense attorneys are terrifically presented but not situated within a cultural framework. Hence the need for this ethnography's attempt is to situate and explain the lived experiences of death penalty defense lawyers within a cultural framework.

It is worth noting that the lawyers who participated in this study gave interviews that in many ways overlap with those from Shaffer's and Gould & Barack's work. That said, there are key distinctions that emerge because of my focus on lawyers in one state as opposed to across the country. For instance, Gould & Barack's work acknowledges that among the lawyers they interviewed, some death penalty defense lawyers were considered by their peers to be substandard, inadequate or ineffective. The Colorado attorneys I interviewed expressed no such feelings toward their fellow death penalty defense attorneys in the state.[76] Most of

---

[72] Supra Footnote 68 at 7.
[73] Id. at 59.
[74] Id. at 52–53 and 60–61.
[75] Id. at 10–11.
[76] To be fair, one attorney named Christopher Nelson did say he felt some of the Colorado death penalty defense lawyers were too self-righteous and even unethical (no specific examples of unethical behavior were provided) but never once indicated they were unqualified.

these lawyers knew each other personally, had worked on cases together, trained younger generations of defense lawyers and continued to collaborate. Importantly, the state of Colorado whether it be through the public defender's office or the alternate defense counsel's office ("ADC") created a system where only experienced murder/homicide defense attorneys are allowed to be lead counsel on a death penalty case and even then the number of 'death penalty qualified' lawyers in Colorado is kept small. By intentionally keeping the number of capital defense attorneys small, only a specific group of people will even be allowed to take death penalty cases and, as I will demonstrate later in this ethnography, it is individuals most amendable to working within a culture of resistance that will end up capital defenders in Colorado.

Another distinction between this ethnographic monograph and the work of Gould & Barack is in the reported motivations from the attorneys themselves for doing death penalty work. Specifically, Gould & Barack talk about how death penalty defense lawyers encompass motivations such as (1) moral conviction, (2) desire for complexity in work, (3) desire for excitement or 'adrenaline rush,' (4) prestige and ambition, (5) oppositional personalities and past psychological trauma and (6) financial gain.[77] I found that the Colorado death penalty lawyers, categorically speaking, have little motivational overlap with the attorneys interviewed by Gould & Barack.[78] For instance, the attorneys I talk with never discuss the work in terms of a financial gain but instead report that while the state provides 'adequate resources' to defend their cases, the prevailing mindset is that if one is not a public defender, these cases are a significant financial burden. Moreover, while some of the attorneys I interviewed discuss how doing capital defense work can provide an adrenaline rush or even an opportunity to do interesting and challenging work nobody set out to be a capital defense lawyer for these reasons. Finally, none of the attorneys discussed wanting to be a death penalty defense lawyer to satisfy their ego and gain prestige within the legal community. I believe these distinctions exist because Colorado death penalty defense lawyers are themselves culturally unique when viewed

---

[77] Supra Footnote 68 at 65.
[78] Id.

among all capital defenders within the nation—hence the need to focus on culture more so than emotional impacts or effects of the death penalty litigation process on those working in the system.

The work of Sheffer and Gould & Barack is incredibly important, rigorous, explanatory, inciteful and in many ways groundbreaking because it sets the standard of what type of responses a person can expect to receive when interviewing death penalty defense lawyers. However, not all states are the same and as such there will be variance in what themes are present when capital defense lawyers are interviewed and the methods they engage in while actively litigating cases. The variances are likely a product of legal cultures—hence the need for a more focused attention on the culture death penalty defense lawyers create within the community they practice law.

Why Study Colorado Death Penalty Defense Lawyers?

Colorado is home to some of the best criminal and capital defense lawyers in the country.[79] The Colorado public defender's office is nationally recognized for creating the "Colorado Method of Voir Dire." The Colorado public defenders office gives yearly trainings to lawyers from all across the country on the Colorado Method of Voir Dire which is considered the gold standard method for selecting jurors in death penalty cases.[80] Moreover, a number of the death penalty defense lawyers I interviewed told me about how they routinely give trainings on litigation strategies across the country. The reputation of Colorado's death penalty defense lawyers as being some of the best litigators in the country is well known but little to nothing is known about them as people or their legal culture.

---

[79] Furman, Patrick (2003). "Wrongful Convictions and the Accuracy of the Criminal Justice System." *The Colorado Lawyer*, 32(9): 11.
[80] https://www.coloradodefenders.us/training/capital-training/.

While there has certainly been work dedicated to understanding how death penalty defense attorneys should be categorized,[81] these projects do not make the culture of death penalty defense lawyers a primary theme. There are plenty of reasons to study the culture of death penalty defense lawyers but there is one that may be more important than others because it is tied to the US Constitution. Namely, the 6th amendment to the US Constitution, which requires people facing the death penalty to be provided "effective assistance from legal counsel.[82]" Some may find it surprising that the bar for determining what behaviors is or is not 'effective assistance' is incredibly low.[83] In fact, legal scholars have argued that defense lawyers provide such little resistance at trial to the securing of death sentences coupled with an "…unwitting connivance of the anti-death penalty bar…police, prosecutors, judges and juries operate with strong incentives to generate as many death sentences as they can-reaping robust psychic, political and professional rewards-while displacing the costs of their many consequent mistakes onto capital prisoners, post-trial review courts, victims and the public.[84]"

There are numerous horror stories about death penalty defense lawyers from states all across the country that courts routinely rule are providing effective assistance of counsel. Take for example *Wilson v. Commonwealth*[85] where the defendant Gregory L. Wilson sat on Kentucky's Death Row for over 28 years, unable to win a new trial, despite his lead trial counsel's drinking problems who, according to co-counsel, "manifested all the signs of a burned-out alcoholic," who's home prominently displayed a large flashing Budweiser sign and his business card listed the phone number for a local bar called Kelly's Keg because the lawyer

---

[81] See generally: Kaplan, Paul (2010). "Forgetting the Future: Cause Lawyering and the Work of California Capital Trail Defenders." *Theoretical Criminology*, 14(2): 211–235; Sarat, Austin and Stuart Schiengold (1998). "Cause Lawyering and the Reproduction of Professional Authority: An Introduction." In: Austin Sarat and Stuart Schiengold (eds) *Cause Lawyering: Political Commitments and Professional Responsibilities*, pp. 3–28. Oxford: Oxford University Press.
[82] Strickland v. Washington, 466 U.S. 668, 692 (1984).
[83] Bright, Steven (1994). "Counsel for the Poor: The Death Sentence Not for the Worst Crime but for the Worst Lawyer." *The Yale Law Journal*, 103: 1835–1883.
[84] Liebman, James (2000: 2032). "The Overproduction of Death." *Columbia Law Review*, 100: 2031–2156.
[85] 836 S.W.2d 872 (1992).

spent the majority of his days drinking there. The Kentucky Supreme Court found Wilson's lawyer did provide effective assistance of counsel—Wilson had his death sentence commuted to Life with the possibility of Parole by former governor Matt Bevin in 2019.[86] One of the more notorious cases comes out of Texas where the trial, appellate and Texas State Supreme Court found that a defendant was not entitled to habeas corpus relief despite the fact his court appointed attorney was falling asleep during critical phases of death penalty litigation—only after the case reached federal jurisdiction and made national headlines was it found that sleeping during trial was deemed ineffective assistance of counsel.[87]

Examples of such lawyering are not confined to death penalty cases. As I am writing this book, the US Court of Appeals for the 6th Circuit found a defense attorney that constructively abandoned their client at trial by not doing any investigation, waiving his opening statement, doing no cross examination of government witnesses and had a closing argument of "I have nothing judge" is, in the court's perspective, effective assistance of counsel.[88] Hence there is a need to understand the culture of resistance created by Colorado death penalty defense lawyers because they have created a cultural environment where such behaviors like those listed above are simply unheard of and unacceptable despite such weak standards as to what is considered 'effective assistance of counsel.'

Lastly, Colorado is important to study in isolation because despite their success as defense attorneys, they practice in a state where citizen attitudes and legal precedents mirror the rest of the country. Colorado citizens, like in most other states, initially favored the death penalty and would change, just like the rest of the country, to be more amenable to LWOP if given the choice.[89] Furthermore, the death penalty in Colorado as in other state and federal jurisdictions survived challenges arguing through the use of empirical data that it is arbitrarily used in violation

---

[86] Wolfson, Andrew (2019). He Was Sentenced to Death after a Scandalous Trial. Matt Bevin Commuted His Sentence." *Courier Journal*, Dec. 10, 2019. https://www.courier-journal.com/story/news/crime/2019/12/10/matt-bevin-commutes-death-sentence-gregory-wilson/4384704002/.

[87] Burdine v. Johnson, 262 F.3d 336 (5th Cir. 2001).

[88] Moss v. Miniard, No.: 21-1655 (6th Cir. Court of Appeals 2023). Recommended for Publication.

[89] Supra, Footnote 11.

of the 8th amendment and administered in a racialized manner in violation of the 14th amendment.[90] Finally, Colorado like a number of other states, created a 3-judge panel so that judges, instead of juries, would decide if a defendant lived or died. The goal of the 3-judge panel was to increase the likelihood for prosecutors to secure a death sentence but the practice would be ruled unconstitutional by *Ring v Arizona*.[91]

Participants, Methods and Layout of This Book

This book is based upon 15 interviews with Colorado death penalty defense lawyers conducted over a two-year period.[92] Nine of the lawyers are pure trial attorneys with no appellate experience, one is an appellate attorney and five work as both trial and appellate counsel. In order to identify potential participants, I used purposive sampling techniques and asked each person interviewed to list other people that did death penalty defense work. I collected a total of 23 names but was only able to interview 15 individuals in the timeframe that was personally available.

Getting access was not all that difficult because I knew a couple of the death penalty lawyers personally and had crossed paths with others while also working as a criminal defense lawyer in Colorado. Being a criminal defense attorney gave me a level of trust among the participants, in part at least, because of our mostly shared cynical ideological perspectives about the criminal processing system as a whole and commitment to fight for people being prosecuted, often unjustly, by government officials. As a result, the attorneys were more willing to freely talk about their lives and perspectives than with someone who could not really understand what it is like to be a criminal defense lawyer due to a lack of lived experience.

---

[90] Supra, Marceau, Kamin and Foglia (2013); Beardsley, Kamin, Marceau and Phillips (2015); People v. Montour, Order [2013-05-02] D-181 (Douglas County District Court, No. 02-cr-782, May 2, 2013).
[91] *Ring v. Arizona*, 536 U.S. 584 (2002).
[92] Holstein, James A. and Jaber F. Gubrium (1995). *The Active Interview*. Sage Publishing: New York.

Each interview session lasted about an hour and a half. During the interviews, I asked open-ended questions of each participant on topics such as their upbringing as kids, life during college/law school, initial work as attorneys, how they got into defending capital cases and their experiences as death penalty defense attorneys. Every person I spoke with was incredibly open, talkative and candid in their responses. All but one participant agreed to have their interview recorded so it could be transcribed. On average, the lawyers I interviewed had 29 years of experience practicing as criminal defense lawyers, all of them are white and 73% are male.

Participants were promised anonymity during the interviews—all names used in this ethnography are pseudonyms. Each participant was told prior to their interview that I was only focusing on Colorado death penalty defense lawyers so it is possible a reader could identify them based on information they gave me about their backgrounds or other statements—only one participant expressed some concern but decided to be interviewed anyway.

Honestly, 15 interviews on its face are a small number for a cultural argument but the reality is there are very few people who actually do death penalty defense work in Colorado. It is estimated that about 550 lawyers nationally, or less than 1% of attorneys practicing in criminal law specialize in death penalty defense work.[93] The 15 participants in this book represent around 3% of all death penalty defense lawyers in the country, so my findings are by no means generalizable nationally. However, as stated above at the end of each interview, I asked each participant to recommend other attorneys to be interviewed. The same names kept coming up. I am confident that there are more than 23 lawyers in Colorado that do, or did, specialize in death penalty defense work. Nevertheless, considering that I kept getting the same recommendations and was able to get 15 of those 23 my results are most likely representative of the death penalty defense lawyers in Colorado.

Looking at the responses from each of the lawyers I have organized this book in a manner that retraces the attorney's journey through their

---

[93] Goodrum, Sarah, Mark Pogrebin and Matthew Greife (2015: 339). "Representing the Underdog: The Righteous Development of Death Penalty Defense Attorneys." *Criminal Law Bulletin*, 51(2): 329–357.

experiences growing up, in college, law school and into the legal profession to show that despite their divergent beginnings they all eventually came together and created a culture of resistance in death penalty litigation. In Chapter 2, I look at the experiences participants had while growing up and in college. Most of the participants were able to identify some type of experience that ideologically opened them up to being questioning and being skeptical of governmental policies and practices. It is this ideological base that makes the participants more willing to engage in active acts of resistance to government policies and practices.

Chapter 3 focuses on the law school experience. Specifically, I look at internships and legal clinics where the participants for this ethnography gained 'real world experience' in the practice of law. During these internships, participants would see how the criminal processing system operates from day to day and over time generally see the system as being racist and a promoter of injustice. These views deepen and become a core belief of the attorneys interviewed when they are surrounded by like-minded people whether they are fellow interns, junior attorneys and supervisors. It is at this time when virtually all of the participants are consistently engaging in active resistance to government narratives through the practice of law.

Chapter 4 focuses on the professional lives of the attorney participants where all of the prior socializing experiences shape their attitudes and beliefs towards clients, judges, prosecutors, the police and society at large. Broadly speaking, the attorneys have become socialized to have anger and resentment towards the entire bureaucratic process allowing for capital punishment while being able to express empathy towards their clients and the families of victims. It is in these chapters that the relational mechanisms necessary for an active and effective legal culture of resistance really become center stage.

Specific to Chapter 4, I argue that empathy and anger serve as the emotional bedrock for creating and sustaining a culture of resistance. Most of the death penalty lawyers in Colorado I interviewed are incredibly empathic to their clients, victims and surviving family members of those who had been murdered. Death penalty defense lawyers recognize the pain and suffering their clients inflict while harboring the moral belief that nobody should be executed. As such, the death penalty defense lawyers express a significant amount of anger towards the death penalty as a mode of punishment. When these two emotional states coalesce they are expressed in the perspectives each lawyer has for those with the power to seek and implement death sentences (i.e., judges and prosecutors) and in their litigation strategy which is the subject of Chapter 5.

Namely, Chapter 5 argues that by and large the attorneys interviewed have resentment towards prosecutors and judges because they see them as partisan adversaries on the same side. In other words, the death penalty defense lawyers generally feel that prosecutors and judges alike are partisans desiring their clients to be convicted and sentenced to death. As such, the death penalty defense lawyers truly believe that in order to fight the narrative that their clients must be executed, they are required to embrace an aggressive and tenacious approach to litigation that would normally be rejected in non-capital cases.

Finally, in Chapter 6, I talk about how a culture of resistance requires significant sacrifice on behalf of those apart of the community. The lawyers I interviewed did multiple death penalty cases over their career and while they were successful it came with a cost. The attorneys I interviewed talk about health problems, relational strains and financial pitfalls that come with doing death penalty defense work. My argument is that in order for a culture of resistance to be created and sustained attorneys need to be aware of and accept the personal costs they will undoubtedly experience.

With any luck, this ethnography will do more than advance theory. It is my sincere desire that this work serves as a platform for other organizations working to end capital punishment—a practice I personally deeply oppose—or simply improve the level of representation to people accused of criminal conduct to create their own cultures of resistance. Most importantly, though I just hope this ethnography, if nothing else, rightly tells the story of the death penalty defense lawyers in Colorado and gives life to their beliefs, courage and commitment to a special version of human dignity and justice that is needed now more than ever. Hearing their stories was humbling and inspiring—telling their stories and how their actions manifested into social change is truly an honor.

2

Seeds of Resistance: Skepticism and Questioning of the Government

If one thing is clear about the vast majority of the death penalty defense lawyers I interviewed, it is that overall these attorneys are by and large non-conformists. Being a criminal and death penalty defense attorney requires active opposition to the narratives, arguments and policies of government bureaucracies, agents and other people in power. Looking specifically at death penalty cases, government agents and bureaucracies are advancing a narrative that people who are guilty of murder need to die at the hands of the state. The death penalty defense lawyer must actively resist these narratives of death in order to save their client's life no matter how reprehensible the murder(s) committed. To be a death penalty defense lawyer often means attracting scorn and vitriol from judges, prosecutors and society at large. Death threats from the public are not at all uncommon. Charles Park, one of the participants in this monograph, summed up the overall role of death penalty defense lawyers nicely during his interview: "We are publicly funded enemies of the state." The willingness of the study participants to be actively resistant enemies of the state does not occur in a vacuum. During my interviews, most of the lawyers discussed a variety of different experiences they had growing up and during college that led them down a path where it is perfectly acceptable to question the government and actively resist governmental demands.

Past research on lawyer socialization is sparse. Within this limited body of work, scholars provide a general descriptive picture about what background characteristics influence a person's decision to go to law school and which area of law they practice within. For instance, Andrew Boon finds that background factors such as whether or not a potential law student is from the middle class, their parents have a college education or a potential lawyer has family members practicing law determines if a person will go to law school.[1] Susan Levin[2] suggests that the decision to practice immigration law is in part influenced by lawyers having a personal connection to their clients because they or their family members were immigrants which creates a strong sense of social solidarity among the immigration bar. Missing from this work is a narrative connecting a lawyer's background experience to the creation of a particular legal culture. The purpose of this chapter is to try and demonstrate how the lived experiences each participant had while growing up and attending college gave them an ability and willingness from an early age to openly question and resist government narratives.

There was very little uniformity in the type or timing of the lived experiences detailed by participants because their backgrounds are highly varied. The commonality between the participants is with the internalization and understanding of their lived experiences that led them to a point where they believe it is acceptable and normal to be openly skeptical and willing to question governmental policies and practices. This skepticism and willingness to question governmental desires rather than simply conform are seemingly necessary components for a person to begin actively resisting government narratives in a courtroom or elsewhere.

I break this chapter up into two sections. The first section will discuss the experiences some of the lawyers had prior to attending college that opened them up, ideologically, to being openly critical of governmental

---

[1] Boon, Andrew (2005: 236–237). "From Public Service to Service Industry: The Impact of Socialization and Work on the Motivation and Values of Lawyers. *International Journal of the Legal Profession*, 12(2): 229–260.
[2] Infra footnote 100.

policies and practices. The second section focuses on the experiences attorneys had while in college where a handful take their first steps in moving from ideological to active resistance of governmental narratives, policies and practices.

Pre-College Years

Some of the participants were raised by civically engaged families that actively engaged in acts of resistance. Clarice Montez a criminal defense attorney with 22 years of experience has litigated numerous murder and death penalty cases, talked about her family influences and the early entrance into political activism:

> *We discussed a lot of politics, um, I wouldn't say that I was necessarily involved, but my parents were pretty, you know, they discussed politics a lot, they discussed with me voting issues. I distinctly remember them, you know, Watergate when I was really small. I remember in the mid '70s my mom marching on Washington to try to get the ERA passed.*
> *Interviewer: Did you take part in any of this marching?*
> *I remember doing it when I was little, I mean, as I became an older teenager my mom and I would go to like rallies on campus, I remember when there was the, like the El Salvador stuff and trying to get CU [University of Colorado] to divest, we would go together to that kind of thing.*

Rita Townsend, an appellate death penalty defense lawyer, had similar experiences with her family and how they involved her in political activism at an early age:

> *I was quite young um, very young, like a toddler, I would go around the neighborhood canvasing [for radical Democrats] and that was a big part of our family life...I think it must have been late '70s, maybe early '80s...we were up there encircling Rocky Flats, um and so a lot of stuff like that when I was in high school...when I was in high school I became sort of a service person...had a board position with [REDACTED] that was a program to help the homeless in Denver and you know we would work at the soup*

> kitchens. I can't remember everything we did it was so long ago. You know, there was always stuff happening, stuff in the community.

Similarly, Ricky Donaldson talked about growing up in a politically active family but unlike Rita and Clarice, his parents were more intellectually engaged with protest movements as opposed to active marchers and participants.

> Both of my parents considered themselves and in fact I think were sort of progressive minded liberals. They were involved in, not marching in the South, but involved with the civil rights movement and supportive of the civil rights movement. So I always had a progressive bend in our house. And my father was an immigrant from [foreign country] and I think he in particular always had a feeling for minority people and discriminated against groups.

William Duggan, much like Ricky Donaldson, talked about how he grew up with political awareness from his mother but his 'political radicalization' would not occur until later on in life and be far more extreme than his parents on a whole. Nevertheless, the early exposure is a base for which radicalization can occur.

> My mom was a, well you know, it's kind of, you know. My first political awareness was my mother, was a Kennedy democrat. OK. And the first thing I was ever aware of was what happened while I was in Japan [as a child – around 10 years old] was the Kennedy/Nixon race…. So you know, we are very, you know, I mean know the political, my mom's a Kennedy democrat, so, but that had nothing to do with me becoming a lawyer or being the way I am because I was way more radial than they were. I mean, my radicalization basically came from being a child of the sixties, being in Ohio, Vietnam War, you name it…

Other participants discussed experiencing historical events as young kids and having to grapple with their meaning in real time even though their families may not have been inherently politically active or minded. Charles Park who has been doing criminal defense and death penalty work for almost 30 years talked about being a teenager during the Detroit

2 Seeds of Resistance: Skepticism and Questioning … 29

riots that occurred in the wake of the assassination of Dr. Martin Luther King Jr.

> *I was in Detroit during the 1967 riots after MLK was assassinated. I took a lot of pictures and was there in the middle of it; didn't burn anything down though! The riots really opened me up and I really sympathized with the grievances that a lot of people had.*

Wyatt Desmond a long-time public defender and death penalty defense lawyer discussed how a multitude of historical moments would impact him as a person.

> *My parents are die hard republicans, I am the black sheep of the family… The biggest impact I have always said on me, I mean I was in second grade when Kennedy was killed. I learned about it from a bus driver because we got out of school early. I wasn't much older when MLK was killed and I wasn't much older when Bobby [Kennedy] was killed. But those were kind of distant things that I didn't quite get but in 1970 Kent State happened…I take it all the way back to watching Vietnam and Kent State. I was fourteen, no thirteen, when Kent State happened. I was astounded that the government of Ohio was allowed to call out the National Guard and kill college students.*

Wyatt also gave away, in a moment during the interview that came off as an unguarded and unintentional, the emotional feeling of being 18 years old in 1974 and having his 1A draft card in hand knowing there would be no more college deferments. He was not drafted but also did not want to talk anymore on how he was feeling at that time other than to say with a lot of strain in his voice "…I had a card."

Peter Reynolds, who grew up in a military family and volunteered to go into the infantry during the Vietnam War [he was later stationed in Berlin, Germany] talked about being upset with his parents about the Kent State shootings despite at the time being a supporter of the Vietnam war and even going to a "Rally for Cally" event while in high school at Fort Benning, GA.

> *I was pissed at my folks, you know, because of, I used to get pissed at my dad because of the Kent State stuff and all but it was more because students had*

died, he didn't, he had a pretty cavalier attitude about it being a military guy. I thought that was bad, that it was against young people.

Later in his interview, Peter told me about how during his time in the Army he had become much more sympathetic to the civil rights movement:

I mean, I loved Martin Luther King. I loved him. I don't know why, I was so young, it's not like I knew that much about him. I knew he was a figure, but I just loved him. Yeah, so, and that's never changed.

Tina Carlson, who has been doing criminal defense and death penalty defense cases for over 20 years talked about how her experiences growing up in the South woke her up to the inequities in the world and not liking what she saw.

I was a military brat…raised as a younger person in [The Deep South] during the '60s so what probably motivated me more than anything in my life was as a little girl, we knew black people, but where we lived, because we lived off base, they didn't associate and at one point and time we had a community pool and they bussed the black kids into the pool and none of my neighbors would swim in the pool anymore because it was 'contaminated.' And so having that awakening about what was going on in the world, wasn't so much that I saw that as a government issue as I did, obviously, a much bigger issue and so that's why I became interested in civil rights…Now, when it comes to the death penalty, that is a combination because the government still sanctions it under the guise that it's the will of the people, so yeah I would say that was a bigger influence on me than anything, just living in the South.

Finally, Brenda Telles discussed how her parents, who were very politically conservative, had sent her to Catholic school and it is that education that had a major influence on her life.

…as far as teaching me to be a good person and you know, not judge, I feel like this is a reason I became a public defender was because of all the stuff the taught me…I probably would not have ended up being a public defender if I didn't have that education.

Although it is not clear from this quote alone how her education enabled Brenda Telles to become resistant to government behavior later statements in her interview help make the point clearer. These statements will be discussed in greater detail later but just for illuminating purposes, Brenda Telles told me that after first getting involved with public defender work as a law student she found herself "naively outraged" at how unjust the criminal processing system could be and upset with the *judgmental nature* of prosecutors and judges. These feelings appear to be deeply connected to the values she learned in Catholic school and continued to embody as an attorney which gave her a basis to resist government characterizations of criminal defendants because they are contrary to her value system.

Each of these early experiences, no matter the context, helps socialize the participants, ideologically speaking, to being capable and willing to openly question governmental policies and practices. Some of the participants were active protesters from a young age while others were angry about government behaviors, actions and policies which led to them questioning their efficacy.

The College Years

For a handful of participants in this book, college was a time and place where they first actively engage in oppositional behavior to governmental bureaucracies and people in power mainly through acts of protest. Of course, not all the participants of this book engage in active protesting while in college. Nevertheless, the act of protest in college for those participants that partook, excluding Clarice Montez and Rita Townsend who grew up protesting and challenging the government, is the first identifiable move from ideological to active resistance of governmental policies and practices.

As previously noted, William Duggan discussed already having a liberal bend but becoming far more radicalized than his parents which of course manifested into direct action against the government:

Yeah, I mean, well, yeah. I fought in riots, you know, against the Vietnam War, you know. So the SDS had a clear political message as far as I was concerned. So I was, yes, I was a total radical... CU was a very leftist place, OK...? I spent every minute trying to get back [to Colorado]. I had hitchhiked out to Colorado in '71 was a sophomore at Ohio State at this time, spent three weeks living in Boulder in a canyon. And you know, the place was very hip. It was very radical, you know. I was here when they did the, there was like a hill riot, you know, back then we liked to riot a lot, OK? So you know, Boulder was a good place to riot, you know it was a good place for you know real leftist political action.
Interviewer: "Did you ever get arrested during the riots?"
Not that I want to talk about.

Ricky Donaldson who grew up in a household with a pretty 'liberal bend' had a similar type of experience in college:

I dropped out [of college the first time] because it was a really crazy time. I didn't buy books, we just protested [the Vietnam war] during the day. And frankly I was getting high too much.

Like William and Ricky, Darrell Kappers protested and talked about just being a rebellious youth during his college years:

I was a bad kid, never got arrested but certainly could have!
Interviewer: "What do you mean by bad kid?"
Oh you know, just running around with my stupid friends, drinking beer, causing problems and stuff like that. Where I grew up, there were no gangs or anything so no real opportunity for "real" trouble; just the kind of rebellious stuff...

Later in the interview, Darrell spoke about the protesting he did in college:

...I was out protesting things like Nuclear Arms and Apartheid in South Africa...I used to like lay down and block traffic and things like that. I look back on it now and then look out. Here at these guys now [occupy wall-street protests] and I'm like, these guys are having so much fun out here and it is cold as all getup but on a nice day like today it isn't so bad as a protester. You

know you're out there messing with the cops and stuff. It is just fun. We used to lay down in Boston and block traffic...

Finally, Larry Dunn told me about his time in college and that he was partying a lot and actively protested against the Vietnam War and other social injustices.

When I was in college I spent most of my freshman year smoking pot, drinking and basically just having a great time…and my grades I guess reflected all of that. So I ended up dropping out for a year and that is when I lived in Hawaii and then I eventually thought that I needed to get back to college.

Later in his interview, Dunn told me about how before dropping out he had also burned his draft card in protest of the Vietnam War.

My whole life is dedicated to fighting against injustice and abusive government. In college I burned my draft card, protested, fought the cops and now I get to go into courtrooms and punch bullies (i.e. government) in the mouth.

Whether it be through protest or excessive partying, college was a place for some participants to take their first step in being actively resistant to government narratives, policies and practices.

Outliers

Not all of the participants discussed having lived experiences that are readily connected to partaking in a legal culture of resistance later in life. Four of the attorneys I interviewed did not discuss any specific lived experiences before or during college that would signify a willingness to ideologically or actively oppose and resist government bureaucracies and people in power. Carl Reese talked about his mundane experiences growing up and never really being in a political household or part of active protesting in college. Carl mostly talked about not liking authority and organizations but never linked it to any specific experience:

> *I always sort of had an anti-authoritarian streak. Just sort of not liking authority, I mean it wasn't anything, the point of, it was just fort of a mild undercurrent in my personality where I think that fit in well...Always have generally had a dislike of sort of organizations, committees, so I mean, you know...I just sort of dislike, I hate committees, I hate the way committees work, I hate the idea of Robert's rules of order. I just don't work well in that capacity.*

Frank Powell and Lewis Frankfurter could not think of any experiences they had growing up or in college that could somehow be attributable to harboring a willingness to openly question and be actively opposed to government bureaucracies, people in power and their policies. Finally, Chuck Nielson for the most part lived a fairly politically conservative and conventional life that led him down the road to being a prosecutor for most of his career—it was not until much later in life, unlike the rest of the participants for this book, that he became a criminal and death penalty defense lawyer. The most Chuck Nielson said about his views on government as a youth was in regard to the resignation of Richard Nixon:

> *Well, I you know, I graduated from high school in '75, which was um, you know, the wind down on uh Vietnam, the uh resignation, Nixon's resignation, those sort of things were going on when I was in high school. And I was always, uh, you know, I was always politically aware. I didn't march on Washington or anything but I knew what was going on.*
> *Interviewer: "What were your opinions generally?"*
> *I'm a conservative republican and I um, but I thought Nixon, he needed to go. It was time to go. I did, I didn't have hatred for Nixon like the left did but clearly he needed to, he needed to be gone.*

Looking at Larry, Carl and Chuck's statements, there is a level of unconventionality to them that is not readily connected to experiences growing up or in college. For Carl Reese, being anti-authoritarian was just part of who he was—albeit there is likely a good reason for his ideology but the fact is he just is not aware of any specific or series of events leading him to his mindset. For Larry Dunn, the heavy partying in college may at some level be interpreted as rebellious but without anything else to connect it to in his interview I am left with seeing it as just a year of behaving contrary to a stereotypical status quo of going to college, getting good grades and graduating on time. In other words, Larry Dunn did things his way. Finally, with Chuck Nielson, his statements about Nixon indicate a willingness at some level to think independently.

Although their lack of identifiable experiences are outliers when compared to the rest of the participants, the statements from Carl, Larry and Chuck indicate at least some ideological principles that are highly amendable to future admittance into a culture of resistance—namely independence in thought and behavior.

Conclusion

Overall, most participants I interviewed were able to discuss various experiences in their lives before and during college which led to being (1) ideologically willing to question governmental narratives, policies and practices and (2) for some to engage in active acts of resistance against governmental narratives, policies and practice through protest. While some of the participants actively engaged in protest while in college, the others who did not would later be socialized into active resistance against governmental policies and practices through clinical and internship experiences in law school. In the next chapter, I focus on how most of the participants, except for Chuck Nielson, partook in an internship or legal clinic where as law students they defended people in court accused of various crimes. It is these experiences early on that seem to fully shape the participant's views going forward after becoming practicing attorneys.

3

The Socializing Experiences of Law School & Internships

During the interviews, I asked the participants about their time in law school. Some participants were ambivalent to the law school experience and others seemed to enjoy taking a wide variety of classes. For example, William Duggan stated *"I went to law school to be a defense attorney. The rest of law school is pretty silly to me, you know? Torts and contracts and corporations, wills and trusts. The only thing I was really interested in was evidence, criminal procedure, criminal law, constitutional law."* Charles Park expressed a similar perspective when he stated *"I only enjoyed criminal law and procedure probably because I knew I was going to be a criminal defense lawyer."*

Other attorneys enjoyed the entire law school experience as opposed to just criminal law and procedure. Darrell Kappers stated: *"I loved law school, I thought it was awesome…it was like wow really this is all I do, read this stuff and talk to people about it and I found it intellectually stimulating and easy at the same time."* Similarly, Rita Townsend simply exclaimed in response to a question about her time in law school *"I loved it!"*

My point here is that much like the variance in the families they grow up in there are a multitude of feelings toward law schools. No matter how they felt about the law school experience the primary commonality shared among the participants is the exposure to the practice of criminal defense through the internship and clinical programs. In Chapter 2, I talk about how the majority of the lawyers had some type of lived experience that makes them amenable to openly criticizing and resisting the acts and policies of government actors. In other words, experience teaches them that it is acceptable, if not necessary, to question and resist the narratives, policies, acts and motivations of people in power. Here in this chapter, I focus on how the law school experience provides each of the participant's opportunities to partake in internship programs which are the primary entry points for most into the practice of criminal law. Of course, not every participant went into law school knowing or even wanting to be a criminal defense lawyer while others had no doubt. For instance, Tina Carlson, Charles Park, Brenda Telles, William Duggan and Darrell Kappers made the decision to practice criminal defense law before going to law school while others such as Larry Dunn, Rickey Donaldson and Carl Reese discussed their initial desires to practice something different such as environmental law. Three of the participants initially worked as prosecutors which is what pushed them into criminal defense work. Despite the different starting points at the beginning of law school, the majority of the attorneys I interviewed told me about how their experiences doing internships or legal clinics re-affirmed or heavily influenced their decision to focus on criminal law and become defense attorneys whether it be through a connection with their personal values or happenstance.

These internships and clinics are significant points in any law student's life because it gives them the opportunity to learn how to practice law through exposure to more experienced attorneys. As Levin[1] points out in her study of immigration attorneys, the practice settings and manner in which people first learn to practice law likely affect their identification with various communities. It stands to reason then that internships and clinical experiences, which are opportunities to learn the practice of law before becoming a licensed attorney, are important points in the socialization process for young lawyers because it is an introduction to legal

---

[1] Levin, Leslie C. (2009). "Guardians at the Gate: The Backgrounds, Career Paths, and Professional Development of Private US Immigration Lawyers." *Law & Social Inquiry*, 34(2): 399–436.

practice and the norms and values held by current practicing lawyers such as public defenders. I structured this chapter by separating the participants into three distinct categories: (1) those that already knew they wanted to be criminal defense lawyers, (2) those that used the internship experience to find where they belong and (3) those that started with the prosecutor's office and learned they belonged working in criminal defense. No matter the category, the aspiring attorneys are exposed to the realities of criminal law and defense work. Overwhelmingly, the participants discuss how this exposure to criminal law and defense work seemed to guide them into working for public defender's offices and thereby become lifelong criminal defense and later death penalty defense lawyers.

Internships for the Criminal Defense Minded

Charles Park told me that during law school, he only enjoyed criminal law classes and knew that he was going to be a criminal defense lawyer so he clerked for the legal aid society and public defender's office and '*absolutely loved working with public defenders.*' Brenda Telles, who was a business administration major in college, told me that after meeting a woman as an undergraduate who was a public defender she decided to become a criminal defense lawyer which caused her to become bored with business.

> *Interviewer: "So during your time in college what about business didn't appeal to you?"*
>
> *"I guess I found it boring. I ended up majoring in business administration despite the fact that I knew I was going to go to law school and be a public defender, so I don't know, I just, you know like I remember ordering the Wall Street Journal and I'm like, "This is killing me, this is so boring" and I think now, looking back, I think I'm a more man interest type of person than a numbers or business person. I realized that somewhere in college an decided well you can go to law school with any degree so I'll just finish up this [business] degree and go to law school, but it was you know, middle of my [college] time where I got hooked up with the public defender so at that point I thought that suits me more than this does."*

Shortly thereafter Brenda talked about interning with the public defender's office and how she felt the very first time going to jail and meeting a client to represent him for a bail hearing:

> *I had never been to a jail, any exposure at all to criminal justice stuff. And so I remember going to the jail and navigating, you know, getting clearance for the jail and getting in, you know, the drama of just going into a jail. It was a little bit scary but you know, like this is interesting. When I got there and sat down and he [the client in jail] was perfectly respectful and nice and I got the information and I went back and I remember thinking, 'well, that wasn't that bad, like he wasn't a monster.'*

A couple minutes later in the interview, Brenda elaborated on trips to jails, meeting with people, and coming to understand how the criminal justice system operated in a manner that solidified her decision to be a public defender.

> *Like, there were no evil monsters on the other side of the sliding door [clients who were incarcerated] and it all worked out fine and the more I worked and the more I was exposed to clients and their cases, the more it really just dawned on me that these are just sort of regular people or sometimes damaged people, but I wasn't running into anyone who was like evil or mean, it was just people who either had made a mistake or people who because of their life circumstances had ended up where they were. I was not scared or wishing bad upon these people and* **it was really enlightening for me to realize these are not bad people, these are just regular people who need help**. *And I also at the time, there was a guy charged with murder and he was in jail and someone else confessed and this guy got out of jail and I distinctly remember asking the lawyers, "well what does he get for being in jail all that time?" And they were like "are you kidding me? What are you ten years old? He gets nothing." You know? And I remember being horrified that someone could be charged and their whole life ruined and they're in jail and they get nothing but a release from jail for that and remember being particular and sort of naively outranged by that and you know, that just shouldn't happen. It sort of motivated me, you know, maybe more people should be doing this sort of work so that happens as infrequently as possible.*

Eventually, I asked Brenda about the influence of her internship experience on becoming a public defender and she stated:

> ...99% of it was the internship and I like the kind of people who became public defenders. They seemed less stuffy, less arrogant, more real life, cussed more, drank more, had really good parties, fun to hang out with, you know, I certainly would not want to be a lawyer who had to behave and so just their, just the public defenders themselves, I don't think I would have become a lawyer before wanting to be a public defender.

Frank Powell is another attorney who, like Brenda Telles, knew that he was going to be a criminal defense lawyer.

> ...Being a criminal defense lawyer. I mean, that was the only thing I wanted to do, I didn't have some notion that law school itself was a good thing, I just wanted to be a criminal defense lawyer.

Powell told me about his views and attitudes which were developed during a criminal defense clinic while in law school and representing actual clients:

> **I've always liked working for the underdog, the criminal defendant certainly is an underdog in the system.** I'm appalled at some of the racism and classism that continues to exist in America and this is one way to fight that sort of thing.

In his interview, Darrell Kappers told me about how he fell in love with the public defender's office while doing internships and couldn't be happier for now being paid to "...kick the man's[2] ass."

> I just remember being interested in getting involved with the PD's office and interned all three years with the PD trial office, including summers and none of it was paid. I did a lot of cool juvenile law stuff during the 94 summer of violence...and I was doing detention hearings where everyday these kids who got arrested and that was when they passed the law saying you could

---

[2] 'Man' is a pseudonym for government.

*hold kids without bail s***o that was a big deal because we were fighting against that; how can you hold a kid without bail but you cannot hold an adult without bail so how does that work right?** *So we were litigating that and whatnot and it was just a cool period and I fell in love with it. It was a perfect fit for me philosophically, politically and it turns of my abilities it fit really really well.*

However, Tina Carlson talked about wanting to be a public defender and while that desire never wanted, it was tested due to experiences with sexism in the office.

What was noticeable to me is that in the public defender system, which I was, I mean I started interning while I was in law school; I was going to be a public defender, there was no doubt about that. But at the time I was interning there were only two female office heads and so management wise, with the public defender system, it was an old boys club.

Tina told me that despite the 'old-boys club' mentality, there was a lot of support between the women who were interns and later hired to be public defenders.

I was in the office with some very strong trial attorneys that were women. And we slowly were getting more supervisory positions, you know we were getting the bigger cases, trying the bigger cases and there was a period of time when the men in the system labeled us 'the committee.' And we were all fairly good looking women – those were the days! We dressed really nice; we were very talented in the courtroom; we had big personalities and we were moving up. And there were probably about ten of us. And maybe even a few more, but the core group, and so they labeled us the committee and talked about us in a negative way…for a while.

Internships for Those Finding Their Way

Certainly, law school is a time and place to explore different areas of law and find out which area is the most interesting and desirable within which to practice. A number of the participants for this book talked about arriving at law school without the immediate desire to be criminal defense lawyers. For instance, Ricky Donaldson initially considered environmental law before interning with the public defender's office.

> *"My degree was in environmental studies, it was the first wave of environmentalism…the notion of being an environmental activist lawyer was appealing to me and you know, there was some subtle family pressure to be a successful guy…so…"*
>
> Interviewer: *"Was there anything in particular with the public defender, when you were interning, that just kind of clicked right away like, 'yeah, this is what I need to be doing?'".*
>
> *"I mean yeah, being a public defender always seemed to me, both in that internship and in the years when I was a public defender, virtually the perfect job. There was the theater of the courtroom, there was the public speaking piece if you liked that kind of thing.* **And at the same time, it's you know, it feels righteous because you're helping poor people. So the combination of factors made it to me, at that time, the perfect job.** *I still look back at it in that way."*

Carl Reese entered law school with the desire to practice environmental law but told me about how over time and with new experiences he switched gears and focused on becoming a criminal defense attorney.

> Interviewer: *"What was it about environmental law that attracted you to it?"*
>
> *"…The cause itself. I always had a fairly strong environmental streak…always had a strong belief in the preservation of wilderness, the you know, we're ruining the world that type of thing, with our growth, our technology. So I would say it was more of an ideological thought but then it was that the practice itself, you know, no matter how much good they do, it's like, it doesn't do you any good if you don't enjoy it…I mean it was fascinating but back in law school and everything, it's not, there isn't a human element out there. It [environmental law] is very statute, massive documents, massive data type of things and I prefer cases that are simpler, easier to understand that have sort of a key human element to it."*

Carl then told me about a clinical program for students interested in criminal law that really seemed to move him off environmental law.

...I was very lucky that a new criminal trial, criminal practice legal aid clinic got added. They got a new professor and they added a trial practice, criminal practice, where you actually had real clients. And signed up for that and that was a god send.

After his clinic program, Carl mentioned a conference he went to and realized that the best group of people for him to work with are public defenders:

> *I remember the public defender's conference is held every year in September and I didn't know, I was walking along and I look in this room and here's all these very sophisticated or well-dressed people that didn't look like what I expected and I figured out that was an insurance sales thing and I keep going down the hall and then here's a much more rag tag group of folks and it was public defenders. And it's like, you know, these are folks I really enjoyed meeting and you know, once you see the whole system come together, you take all the classes, **you see the sort of passion for representing the dispossessed**. So that was a fairly cementing event.*

Shortly thereafter, Carl told me that he was offered a paid internship outside of criminal law but instead begged the public defender's office to keep him as an unpaid student worker for the remainder of law school—they agreed and hired him after graduation.

Rita Townsend is another, like Carl Reese and Ricky Donaldson who initially went into law school with a desire to work on environmental issues. Rita specifically told me that her focus was on environmental justice. However, the initial internship for her was not a motivating experience.

> *I split the summer between the state department and the justice department. Half the summer in the office of environmental affairs in the DOJ which was awful. I thought it would be really interesting and it was dead. It was the worst office, they were all, all they were doing was like civil law suits involving like radiation experiments the government had conducted on people many years ago and some other line of disgusting civil suits and everybody there was beaten down and board...I hated everything about it. It was awful.*

3 The Socializing Experiences of Law School & Internships

Towards the end of law school, Townsend still did not really know which area of law she wanted to work within. Eventually, she began working as a law clerk for a large law firm doing pro-bono litigation where she got a first taste of criminal law and death penalty defense work.

I actually worked on a capital habeas appeal, pro-bono, which I found fascinating and that was probably the very beginning for me of where I am now. Getting familiar with all the issues and realizing what atrocious injustices occur in capital habeas cases. I was working with a lawyer who was involved with the Coleman v. Thompson case, which is the, you know, the petition [for habeas] that was filed was a day late, procedural default case. It was not the lawyer's fault, she had bailed that case out subsequent to the default and had taken it to the Supreme Court, but she was very influential on me, had worked at the ACLU before Arnold and Porter. She gave me a sense that the death penalty was an area that smart lawyers needed to spend time working on that there was a gap and she sort of planted that idea in my head um, and at the time I was thinking, yo know, OK so if I go to a big law firm there's all this neat pro bono work that I can do, so maybe I should think about that.

Rita did think about doing death penalty work and began handling death penalty habeas corpus claims for a few years in private practice before becoming a federal public defender.

Peter Reynolds went to law school not really sure what he wanted to do and after being in a property law class became "*a miserable guy because I did not like law school....I think as an institution and intellectual pursuit its a wonderful, nuanced, foundational thing but I wouldn't say that it was for me.*" However, it was after meeting a well-known public defender (a good number of participants talked about working with and being influenced by this individual) and interning with the public defender's office that Reynolds figured out where he should look for a home within the law.

[He] was one of those guys who had been rounded up and stuck into FRK stadium or whatever they called it during the Pentagon riots and demonstrations – he was a fervent little son of a bitch. I heard him talk and I thought, I think that's what I want to give a go. He mentioned that they have work

study...*I went and applied as quickly as I could get down there...That's what I did, I went down and applied and got in there.* **And it became home. Just like that.**

Peter Reynolds' experience is unique because while doing the work study he assisted on a death penalty defense case. This experience really solidified his desire to be a defense attorney and to later do death penalty defense.

> *There was a nasty death penalty case going on...This guy [REDACTED], just, he'd done, really fucked up this woman pretty badly...I ended up doing a bunch of background stuff. We were going to juror homes, spotting,*[3] *we'd get the list and go and see what kind of bumper stickers they had and all that and I transited around with my girlfriend, on weekends took, and that for a while and you know, believed in the cause.* ***I mean, I really did and it became more and more exciting, the thought of sort of being in things that had a lot of negative publicity associated with them and kind of being, standing beside folks who really needed it, you know? Being the one who was willing to do it. And it just took hold.***

Similarly to Peter Reynolds, Wyatt Desmond did not initially know he was going to be a public defender until taking a criminal law class and later interning with a public defender's office. Before interning Desmond talked about his first experiences in law school, specifically his first day of class, and wondering if he could even make it to graduation.

> *Well he [law professor] thought he was the Paper Chase*[4] *guy. So he is going to fuck with us the first day and this is what he does. He sent out the preliminary reading assignments and we had to prepare two cases. And we had to prepare the plaintiff and the defense side. I don't know what the hell this is supposed to look like. So I spent hours on handwriting, there weren't, we didn't have laptops, we didn't have computers, right. I'm handwriting my briefs and he calls, he had everybody's name and so he would randomly select and you*

---

[3] It is important to note that nothing illegal was occurring by the lawyers or law student. They were trying to do juror research without physically contacting jurors to see if there was anything visible to indicate that they would be biased in favor of a death sentence.

[4] Reference to movie "The Paper Chase". https://www.imdb.com/title/tt0070509/

would have to stand up and make the presentation. So we walk in the first day, supposedly he's randomly selecting, this guy gets up and does this amazing presentation then he calls another name and this lady gets up and she does this amazing presentation. I'm going, "I have zero chance of surviving law school" because I don't have any of that shit in here. We get to the 49th or 50th minute of class and he introduces them, one was his third year grad student and one was a practicing lawyer – he brought them in just to scare the shit out of us which he succeeded in doing. My second class was property. We spent the entire session on the preface of the book. And well, I am not smart enough to get through law school but then we hit criminal and constitutional law and it was just, that's where I wanted to be. Those are the things that were interesting to me.

Shortly after telling me this, Wyatt talked about doing multiple internships under the student practice act and being able to represent clients even as a law student. Wyatt then told me about how it was taking the things he learned about practicing law back to class that really kept him going down the road of being a public defender.

There were only two of us [students in class] that were working at the PDs office and we would go back and we'd talk in our criminal procedure who I still remember, we were talking about bail and he wants to talk about the constitutional right to bail and we're going, 'It ain't working that way down there professor.' You know, we're going in the back of the cell, where the, in the holding cell where the guys just pissed down the front of his pants and the judge isn't setting the bail that anyone can get out on and the pressor gets like pissed because he doesn't want to hear it because that's not how it's supposed to work. And we're going, but that is how it's working...And so, I couldn't wait to get out of law school because I wanted to do the real law, not hear about it.

Louis Frankfurter is another one of the attorneys that did not know he was going to become a criminal defense attorney. It was the combination of classes and internships that truly motivated him to become a public defender.

I became interested in criminal law and constitutional law courses. I had a very good professor in those areas and I became interested in them. We also had a really good trial practice program run by a lawyer named '[REDACTED] and between trial practice, criminal law and constitutional law I developed an interest in those areas. It helped because after my first year I got some grant, I don't remember what it was, maybe LAAA grant, and there was a bunch of us who got paid to actually go do an internship with either the district attorneys or public defenders office anywhere in the country. Out of the ten of us I was one who chose the public defender's office which had just been established and was quickly gaining a national reputation and that further developed my interest in criminal law. It didn't hurt that they offered me a job at the end of the summer either! So I went back, finished my last two years, graduated, came back and took the job they offered me.

Interning with the Prosecutors Then the Defense

Chuck Nielson, Clarice Montez and Larry Dunn all worked as interns for either a state or federal prosecutors office. Chuck Nielson remained a prosecutor for a number of years before going into private practice as a criminal defense lawyer. For Chuck, the move had nothing to do with morals or being dissatisfied with the job itself—as he put it in the interview a time came when it was just time to leave. Clarice and Larry would learn from their experiences with prosecutors offices that they simply did not belong in that community of lawyers.

For Larry Dunn, the internships with prosecutors early on in law school before interning with the public defender's office exposed him to a practice and set of values and norms that were at odds with his own:

> "When I was at the DA and US Attorney's office I thought you know these guys are just a bunch of stiffs, these guys are not the kind of people I want to go out and have a beer with not that any of them would ever want to go out and have a beer you know, I mean these are just, these *prosecutors are just not my type of people* but at the public defender's office I realized that these are my kind of people…"
>
> Interviewer: "So was your mindset different when you were with the prosecutors?"

3 The Socializing Experiences of Law School & Internships

> "Well, it was, well I mean politically correct students at [REDACTED] in 1977 were all about being criminal defense attorneys and that prosecutors suck and I never took that position.[5] I always thought no, prosecutors have an important role in society and that, well, there are people out there who do need to be off the streets."

For Dunn, this mentality would begin to change when tasked with prosecuting a man who was homeless, living in a park and allegedly "took a swing" at a police horse.

> *I was agonizing over offering the guy a plea bargain in the case or not because I wasn't sure I believed these cops and my buddy [a public defender representing the accused] was telling me "Look, what is this guy supposed to do? He is getting hassled by these cops and this is where he lives so what is the guy going to do? What are you going to do, put him in jail for this?" I thought to myself well, I can't put this guy in jail but I was agonizing over a proper deal…Should I have this guy stay out of the park for 30 days or 10 days or what should I do and then I got to thinking well I wasn't there so why, well you know are we gonna take this to trial, this is well I guess really disturbing to me that I wasn't there, I can't say this guy is guilty and then here I am, Mr. Law Student trying to craft a punishment for this guy; you know, I'm not his daddy, I'm not his mommy and I'm not sure what happened; who the hell am I going in and inflicting pain and suffering on this guy;* **this is not who I am as a person so I uh, you know, it was difficult. The whole mindset of being in the prosecutors office was difficult. But if I had not experienced it I wouldn't have known so it really was one of the best things I did in law school.**

Dunn would go on to tell me: "*I eventually worked at the [REDACTED] Public Defender's office and after just a brief time I knew that is exactly where I needed to be.*" Clarice Montez's internship with a US attorney's office had a similar effect.

---

[5] As you will see later in this book Larry Dunn's tone toward prosecutors changes dramatically and to the critical.

"During law school...I had a friend who had gotten me an internship at the U.S. Attorney's office so I did that for a summer, more than a summer, a year. And I realized that was the opposite of what I wanted to do."

Interviewer: "Why was that?"

"Well for a lot of the prosecutors I felt that what they were doing was sort of a game of outwitting the defense lawyers, opposed to trying to help somebody and I wrote a brief one time basically uh, opposing a guy in prison's pro-se, post-conviction, yeah and the tenth circuit quoted my brief basically word for word in their opinion and um, **I remember thinking if this is a victory, you know, that I beat a guy in prison whose probably got an IQ of about 85, this is not how I want to win any victories and um, basically decided that was not for me and switched into criminal defense.** I did a criminal defense internship and legal aid which was a big influence and then I was lucky enough to be hired by the public defenders office when I graduated."

Interviewer: "OK, so it wasn't like a moral opposition to working with prosecutors in the U.S. attorney's office, it was just more of 'not a good fit?'

"**Well, I think there was a moral evolution because eventually and yeah, I think that was a moral thing for me.** I, I just couldn't live with myself really trying to keep people in prison who you know didn't have the same advantages in life that I did, uh, mental illness, uh intellectual disabilities, that was something I realized that I couldn't do."

Conclusion

Taking all the interviews into account, there is no doubt that the internship and clinical experiences each of the lawyers went through served as reinforcement or an influence to become criminal defense attorneys. Thematically, the interviews in general demonstrate that the lawyers I interviewed were put in a position where they really had a cause to fight for—namely helping people in need or as Carl Reese put it "..._seeing the sort of passion for representing the dispossessed, that was a really cementing moment for me._"

Clearly, not every lawyer took the same path to end up with a deep desire to help people in need and certainly criminal defense work is not the only area of law where the 'dispossessed' are desperate for legal representation. In fact, it is possible that had these lawyers done a different internship or been able to do more active and human centered work in law school or during internships they could have ended up being environmental activist lawyers or something else. This is the power of an internship experience that provides a space for people willing to question and resist government narratives to live their values every day. All of these lawyers went to top law schools and could have made major salaries working in the private sector but the internship and clinic experience gave them the opportunity to pursue a desire to help people and importantly, help people whose perils are connected to government practices.

As the interviews of Brenda Telles, Darrell Kappers, Clarice Montez, William Dunn and Wyatt Duggan explicitly demonstrate, they saw firsthand how the real world practice of criminal law and the power wielded by the government in this arena created inequities and injustices. As I discuss in Chapter 2, these are people who are already pre-disposed and willing to openly question government behaviors and practices. Criminal defense work seemed to be a perfect area for each of the participants to help people in need all while being able to question and fight against government behaviors and practices that cause injustice and social inequity.

4

Empathy & Moral Anger: The Emotional Components of a Legal Culture of Resistance

In the introduction to this monograph, I pointed out that manifest acts of resistance are presumed to be an expression of hope for major and radical social change. Analyses utilizing the culture of resistance framework then should attempt to reveal the implicit reasons to fight against forces engaging in domination and submission. In the context of death penalty litigation, it is prosecutors that choose whether or not to activate a legal process that seeks to secure the execution of another human being; this process which is openly hostile towards death penalty defense lawyers[1] is overseen and managed by judges. Simply put, prosecutors activate legal processes and judges manage proceedings that every citizen is commanded to respect and obey, no matter how cruel or inefficacious, as a matter of duty.[2] Within these legal proceedings, prosecutors are routinely referred to as 'The People.' Allowing prosecutors to be referenced as 'The People' is a form of linguistical conscription where citizens

---

[1] Sarat, Austin (1996). "Narrative Strategy and Death Penalty Advocacy." *Harvard Civil Rights and Civil Liberties Law Review*, 31: 353–380.

[2] *Kansas v. Ventris*, 556 U.S. 586, 594 (2009) citing *Michigan v. Harvey*, 494 U.S. 344, 369 (1990).

that do not support the decisions, desires or arguments of prosecutors are forcefully submitted into unification with a legal process working in apparent contradiction to their social will. Defense lawyers and their clients must also submit and operate within this legal processes of which they have no control over in terms of activation or management. As such, prosecutors and judges should be conceptualized as the forces of submission and domination.

Overall, the work I found on capital defense attorneys suggests that most, but not all, death penalty defense lawyers are cause lawyers working[3] to save their client's life and end the use of capital punishment. By and large, death penalty defense lawyers possess deep moral opposition to capital punishment which makes their jobs highly emotional when working within a process that is operating in contradiction to their deep moral sentiments.[4]

While lawyers are expected to provide 'zealous advocacy' for their clients, there is reason to believe that being emotional as opposed to emotionless may be the best way to effectively litigate a case.[5] Emotionally speaking, research suggests that with death penalty defense lawyers being able to connect empathetically with their clients, families of victims and broader society, the attorneys are better able to tap into a deep moral opposition and anger they have towards capital punishment and thus better able to save their client's life.[6] Empathy and anger are important emotional components within a culture of resistance because as I will argue below, they serve as an emotional catalyst to fight the governmental narrative advocating for the execution of their client.

---

[3] Sarat, Austin (1998). "Between (the Presence of) Violence and (the Possibility of Justice: Lawyering Against Capital Punishment." In: Austin Sarat and Stuart Schiengold (eds) *Cause Lawyering: Political Commitments and Professional Responsibilities*, pp. 317–346. Oxford University Press: Oxford. Kaplan, Paul (2005). "Forgetting the Future: Cause Lawyering and the Work of California Capital Trial Defenders." *Theoretical Criminology*, 14(2): 211–235.

[4] Greife, Matthew J., Mark Pogrebin and Sarah Goodrum (2021). "Anger and the Emotional Culture of Death Penalty Defense Lawyers." In: Jake Phillips, Chalen Westaby, Andrew Fowler and Jaime Waters (eds) *Emotional Labour in Criminal Justice and Criminology*. Routledge Publishing: New York; Goodrum, Sarah, Mark Pogrebin and Matthew J. Greife (2015). "Representing the Underdog: The Righteous Development of Death Penalty Defense Attorneys." *Criminal Law Bulletin*, 51(2): 329–357.

[5] Mihai, M. (2011). "Emotions and the Criminal Law." *Philosophy Compass*, 6(9): 599–610.

[6] Supra Gould and Barak (2019).

Emotionally speaking, empathy and anger are why death penalty defense lawyers fight the forces of submission and domination in the hope for radical change in that capital punishment will be abolished.

Empathy in Death Penalty Defense Work

Abbe Smith wrote that a major reason she works to defend people accused of criminal conduct is because "…I am drawn to people in trouble." Sometimes that draw caused her to literally fight in defense of other people such as her sister who were being bullied but as a lawyer, the fighting is done in a courtroom. Smith later wrote "I feel for people in distress. It doesn't matter who they are. The fact that they are in trouble is what makes me want to defend them.[7]"

Empathy is broadly understood as our capacity to grasp and understand the mental and emotional lives of others.[8] According to Krznaric, empathy is the act of "Stepping into someone's shoes, gaining an understanding of their feelings and perspectives and using all of that information to guide our actions.[9]" Defense attorneys are the ones who, far more than judges, prosecutors and the police, step into the shoes of not just their clients but all of those affected by a crime including victims and their families and community stakeholders. This is not done purely for strategic purposes. As Smith points out, a key trait for any defense lawyer is forgiveness which allows for attorneys to "take in and respect the client….[10]"

Sheffer's study of appellate death penalty defense lawyers highlights the role of empathy in that the attorneys largely felt that their emotional relationship with the clients is among the most important part of their

---

[7] Smith, Abbe (2013: 163–164). "How Can You Not Defend Those People?" In: Abbe Smith and Monroe H. Freedman (eds) *How Can You Represent Those People?* Palgrave MacMillan: New York, NY.

[8] Lanzoni, Susan (2018: 3). *Empathy: A History*. Yale University Press: New Haven, CT.

[9] Krznaric, Roman (2014: x). *Empathy: Why it Matters and How to Get It*. Perigee Publishing: New York.

[10] Id., at 169.

work.[11] Prior work strongly suggests that the ability of death penalty defense lawyers to empathize with their clients, and other stakeholders in the capital punishment arena, is an important component in being able to 'personalize' their clients to juries in order to secure life sentences instead of having their client sentenced to death.[12] Empathy does more than help these attorneys relate to their clients. Empathy gives each of the death penalty defense lawyers the ability to connect with juries and other stakeholders such as the families of victims—the ability to connect with people other than their clients is a necessary attribute because these lawyers have to convince a death qualified jury[13] to spare a murderer's life. This of course does not mean death penalty defense attorneys condone or somehow ignore[14] the harm their clients cause by committing a brutal murder—as the proceeding section will show quite the contrary is true. If anything, the defense lawyers I interviewed seem to possess a very balanced amount of empathy because of their ability to understand why their clients commit such brutal murders without going so far as to ignore the feelings of those directly impacted by a killing or slip into a willingness to discount or even condone their client's behavior.

Of all the interviews I did, Clarice Montez spent a great deal of time talking about her duty and the empathic component of her work. Her interview probably provides the best overall description of what some of the lawyers interviewed were trying to convey not just about their clients, but the families of victims who have been brutally murdered.

---

[11] Supra Sheffer (2013: 149).

[12] Id. See also: Berman, D. and S. Bibas (2008). "The Heat Has Its Value: The Death Penalty's Justifiable Persistence." *Faculty Scholarship at Penn Law*, 229. https://scholarship.law.upenn.edu/faculty_scholarship/229; Lynch, Mona and Craig Haney (2014). "Emotion, Authority and Death: (Raced) Negotiations in Capital Jury Deliberations." *Law & Social Inquiry*, 40(2): 377–405.

[13] Infra footnote 13 in Chapter 1 for an understanding of a death qualified jury.

[14] Critics of having too much empathy when defined as "the act of coming to experience the world as you think someone else does" are concerned that it might come at the expense of other cognitive processes such as deliberative reasoning and thus lead to unjustifiable forgiveness. See generally: Bloom, Paul (2016). *Against Empathy: The Case for Rational Compassion*. HarperCollins Publishing: New York.

"Well, I have to save my client's life, I mean, there's a human being stuck on death row that needs me, um, you know, I can't let them die. It's my duty, I mean, it's my duty to do erecting I can to keep that from happening…"

Interviewer: I understand, uh, now when you say the word 'duty' are you, for you is it more of the legal duty that you have to your client or is there really more of a, well do you feel like it's more of a personal moral duty?".

"Well, I mean there is the legal duty, but I do feel like it's my moral duty, yeah."

Interviewer: "Which one do you feel is stronger for you?"

"Moral, but the legal one is pretty strong too."

Interviewer: "OK, now going to the actual clients themselves, um, how do yodel with working closely and possibly even getting to empathize and care for people who are accused of horrible things?"

"…I mean you represent everybody and you don't look at what they're accused of, you deal with the human being. You know, I am one fo those people that believe there is a person who is all bad. Um, I don't believe in evil, and I knock on wood, for the most part, I have really good relationships with clients over the years, um, you know, I just don't guy the government's picture of who they are. I don't think any decent defense lawyer does, but especially if you do death penalty work, you can't, I mean, you'd lose if you do that."

Interviewer: "So you feel it's very important to, not just to know your client for, you know the defense aspect of it, the professional side of it, but to be able to empathize?"

"It's necessary because you're, you know, a person on death row has very little, um, all they have is, you know, often times, they're there because they have tortured relationships with their family, uh, horrible backgrounds, limited uh education, often limited intellectual ability and because of where they are they have little contact with the outside world and their lawyers have to develop a relationship with this person just for the humanity of um, you know, being able to give that person a connection to the outside world, your client, and it helps the case too. Your client is not going to be able to trust you or take your recommendations about what to do in the case, um, if you don't have a really strong bond, that's I think really necessary for uh, it's necessary for any client but especially for a client who's on death row."

Later in the interview, I asked Clarice Montez about her thoughts and feelings that society at large often accuses defense lawyers as being apologists or even claim they do not care about the families of those who have been murdered and if she feels this is unfair.

> *Yeah, I do think that's unfair because we do care about the families. We just by nature of our, the way our system is setup, can't have the kind of relationship with them that maybe would be optimal. Um, anytime, anytime someone is killed, or suffers some horrible devastation, is um, you know, that's a detriment to everybody in our society. Um, frankly I don't think you can do death penalty work, defending people who are accused of horrible crimes and trying to save their life if you don't believe that life is very precious. Uh, and, so I guess I think it would be nice if we had better street cred with the victims' families, um, because of all the death penalty lawyers I know all of them are very concerned about victims families and the pain that they've gone through, um, and uh, you know, you know...I think all of us on some level have made attempts to reach out to victims and families, you know, they're in a particular situation that, they're either more or less receptive to that kind of reach out.*

Montez's interview demonstrates that she, like most of the other lawyers I interviewed, empathically connect with their client while also empathizing with families of victims and society even if nobody recognizes such a reality.

Empathy and the Client

Virtually, every lawyer I interviewed talked about how they, at some level, come to empathize with their clients which seems to be a natural part of the defenders' personalities and an essential component in being able to convince prosecutors, judges and juries to spare a murderer's life. It was not uncommon for a death penalty defense lawyer to even say they came to like their clients that have committed horrible murders. For instance, Carl Reese said in his interview "*I really began to like my clients, understand them.*" Christopher Nelson, the former prosecutor who was the only person I interviewed that did not morally oppose the death penalty said he felt sympathy for his clients—although he is actually describing empathy as opposed to sympathy—looking at a possible execution:

> *I've presented people who were seriously mentally ill, and uh, who I felt very sorry for because of the demons they were battling. Um, I've represented people who had horrible upbringings, um so yeah, I felt sympathy for that.*

The primary manner in which the empathic relationship between client and lawyer begins is when the attorneys recognize at the onset of representation that their clients are not inherently 'evil' as was stated above in Clarice Montez's interview. The death penalty defense lawyers expressed this 'lack of inherent evil' of their clients with a myriad of mantras such as 'nobody wakes up wanting to ruin their life,' 'a person is not the sum of all their bad acts,' and 'a person is not to be seen and judged simply by the worst thing that they do.' From here, the lawyers are able to better connect because it helps them reconcile the reality of a horrible murder being committed by a person they need to essentially humanize so people will consider their lives worth saving.

In her interview, Brenda Telles told me about the reaction she has when first meeting with clients that have committed a death penalty worthy homicide.

> *You know, the cases are disturbing and again I read the discovery and I'm horrified and I go meet the person and I'm like, I can't connect the two, I can't connect that you would have done this if you did do it. I've always felt that way, I still feel that way. It's often very hard to believe that they've done what they're accused of because unless they're really, really damaged, meaning mentally ill or super addicted to drugs or something where I'm thinking yeah, they could do it, I'm sure that he could have done that, but I always attribute it tow whatever problem they're facing…I was told one time that 'no one wakes up in the morning and thinks, oh I think I'm just going to ruin my life today.' When people kill people or do something horrendous, they unlikely have sat down, contemplated it, made that decision anyway. It's usually motivated by mental illness or drugs or depression or frustration or anger or outrage or hate or whatever. But rarely do people, you know, like wake up and thinks this would be a good day to ruin the rest of my life. I've found that to be true in what I've observed. No one wants to be where they are when they're my*

client. *They didn't set out there, they had other plans for their life and you know, things just turned to a mess somewhere and for some reason.*

Tina Carter told me that she still visits some of her clients that are doing life sentences. One she goes and see's every year on his birthday. Others, she will visit and/or correspond with when the write. One of the cases Tina told me about with a client she corresponds with involved a killing that appeared to be racially motivated and as such the death penalty was pursued but the case eventually ended with LWOP.

"[REDACTED] was so abused and over the years, I think, I developed skills that we all have to in the public defender's office to bond with people. And I bonded with him almost like a mother would with a kid because he was so underdeveloped. He was only nineteen and suffered from bi-polar, but he'd never had a mother and he'd been in and out of institutions. He'd been locked up and I had, when I was in [REDACTED], I started a relationship with a young girl in the big sister program and she was housed where he was incarcerated...she also suffered from bi-polar and so, it was, and interestingly enough she was black and [REDACTED] and I talked a lot about her. And deep down he wasn't a racist, he was an abuse person and there' sa great book and we used in in our presentation by giving it to our psychologist on how kids become affiliated with these white supremacist groups, and I learned so much about white supremacy, we went to New York and met with people, we learned everything there was about these movements...Anyway, this stuff talks about these lost kids and how they become, there is a Racist Mind...so it wasn't because he was hateful at all, and he responded to me so well over the years...he was like a little son to me, or a little brother."

Interviewer: "So how frustrating was it for you to really learn the true background of your client, really get underneath and see that he's not nearly as evil as he comes off in the media?"

"He wasn't evil at all. He honestly...he was such a vulnerable. And you know, he's nineteen and he was a serious alcoholic and drug user, so the research shows that they don't, one you start becoming abused, the substances, you don't mature any more. So he's probably, even though he was nineteen, it was like dealing with a fourteen year old I'd say. That was the mentality, so I saw him as a child. Who can hate a child?"

Chapter 5 will talk more about the role of what lawyers refer to as mitigation packages play in litigation and convincing prosecutors, judges and juries to give a LWOP sentence over death. However, it is worth at least mentioning that the empathic connection between Tina Carter and her client is a necessary building block in being able to create a mitigation package that led to a LWOP sentence. Specifically, Tina told me the following:

> [REDACTED] at first blush, is the kind of person you would seek the death penalty on because he stands for things that, you know, we don't want this country standing for. But that's not how the case played out. How the case played out was that this poor, pathetic little bipolar kid who was so abused, and we documented it so well that, well it no longer became about race, it became about mental illness…the DA ended up backing off on this one.

The key here is that empathy is not inherently strategic—as Carter points out, it is a skill she and others develop in order to bond with the client in a way to represent them better. This bonding, and the ability to truly understand her client's past, was a necessary component in showing that a person who, on its face, appeared to commit a racially motivated murder of a beloved community member is not inherently evil.

The empathic connection between the client and defense attorney can be so strong that when a death penalty case is lost and the person goes on death row the emotional toll for the lawyer can be tremendous. For instance, Wyatt Desmond told me that he almost quit practicing law after a death sentence.

> I almost quit after I lost [REDACTED]. You know, I mean, I heard a lawyer say once and it's true, we should actually feel sorry for the prosecution. They spend their entire life looking at and looking for the bad in people. Their worst day, their worst attribute. We spend years with our clients, seeing the good. [REDACTED] is a good example. [REDACTED] was from Compton. I spent two weeks in Compton doing mitigation. It was right after the whole Rodney King blow up. I mean, we're interviewing folks in their living room with helicopters flying over and with them if you hear a car backfire, hit the ground. And that's the kind of interviews we were having to do. The point is, every Friday night there was a show on MTV called Yo Raps. I watched

Yo Raps every Friday night. I knew nothing about rap, I'm a white gy from the Midwest. But it gave me something to talk to [REDACTED] about on Monday. And I'd go in every Monday and we'd talk music. He wasn't a bad guy – he did a bad thing. And that's where people get confused. They only look at the crime, they don't look at the why. Why did this happen? How did he get here? So I get very close. When we lost [REDACTED] I took a week off and just went fly fishing. I was going to quit the system, I was going to quit doing death work. It almost killed me emotionally and it was, I finally came to the conclusion that I wasn't going to let fucking prosecutors run me out of this So I came back and took on the death work for the state.

It is clear that empathizing and getting to know the client in death penalty defense work is incredibly important but not always easy. In his interview, Lewis Frankfurter told me that sometimes it was difficult to work with clients facing the death penalty.

Well, you get to know them, or you should be, better get to know them very well...We know that they are going to have various personality disorders, maybe even some axis one[15] issues. We know that their families are going to be difficult...and so we try to help, I try to help them understand the process that they're in and ultimately help me develop and present mitigation. That's a pretty tall order with some of these clients...You just don't ever get cooperation from many of them and the death penalty lawyers just have to expect that and deal with it...You keep trying and you do your own thing. You don't give up. Sometimes, another member of your team can get through to them, even if you can't. And so sometimes, in one case I used an investigator, one of the members of my team, who seemed to hit it off a little bit and the client, just a little. So we sent her back, time and time again and she finally got through to the guy and he was able to actually make a statement in mitigation at the sentencing phase. Was a though, tough guy. Tough gang member who you never would have thought, ever, would say I'm sorry about anything. But he actually did and it wasn't me, it was this investigator that just kept going back and going back for weeks. So it's really, it's a fascinating process. But for those clients, that's a success story. There are others where there is never success getting through to the client, they just never cooperate with you.

---

[15] Axis one from the DSM.

Rita Townsend talked about the difficulty of working with clients whom she does not connect with empathically but nevertheless, it is still important to try and know everything about the client to represent them the best and save their life.

> *I am not attached to all of my capital clients. There's a couple that I really don't like very much and I don't feel close to. And I find those cases harder than the ones where I am attached. And I think capital work is, it's not unique, I think this is true in any criminal case, but it's magnified because of the stakes in a capital case. You really need to know everything about your client in a capital case to do it right. And you should know. I mean, if the capital case has been done right then the investigation has given you an almost complete picture of who your client is form his multi-generational fleece and his mental health issues and what's happened to him and um, what he's like and why he is the way he is and why he's done what he's done. I think it's hard to know that much about somebody and not get some what attached to them.*

Darrell Kappers told me that it is almost impossible to not empathically connect with a client even if they are not always the easiest to work with.

> *"…It is just us against the world so you have to bond in effect. I find them difficult sometimes and I don't fall in love with them."*
>
> *Interviewer: "So it isn't all that hard to care for someone who has done such terrible things to deserve a death case?"*
>
> *"You would think it is hard but it doesn't seem to be a problem with me and everyone always says that 'how do you represent these people and how do you talk to them?' I think it is because this is what we do; we realize they are humans and incredibly broken and done terrible things but I don't think a person is defined by the worst thing we have ever done and nobody should be. The fact you have committed a horrible crime doesn't define the entirety of who you are. This is what we try to communicate to jurors and to prosecutors in trying to convince everyone not to give the death penalty because things don't happen for no reason at all you know…Most people are brought up with two parents and never beaten and anally raped when I was 5, never abused or neglected and made to eat shit and roll around in dog crap on the floor or abandoned by my family. I have an education and family that*

supported me with a social structure and had everything given to me so the most culpable are the ones who have no real excuse. You have to take that into consideration when deciding if we should kill them or send them to prison for life."

Difficulties in working or connecting with some clients seem to be an exception to the general rule that the lawyers empathically connect with their clients. Empathy with the client does more than just serve as a way to defend a client, it can even be a way to sustain one's self in such high stakes litigation as Ricky Donaldson told me in his interview:

I think what allows someone to do this for decades, which is how long I've been doing it, you have to have some compassion for people. Even people that make mistake sand that make serious mistakes and kill somebody, but there's other decent parts of them. So I can't think of one client over the years, murder case or not frankly, that was a total sociopathy without redeeming features and qualities. I mean, these are human beings that I'm representing and you either can see the humanity and vulnerability in people and then you can do this job for a long time or you can't and then you gotta find a different job.

Empathy, Victim's Families and Society

Primarily the attorneys I interviewed talked in depth about their empathic connections with clients but it did not mean they lost perspective of the serious harm their clients had caused. In fact, it appeared from the interviews that at some level, the lawyers really did feel terribly for victims and their families. Moreover, at no point did a single lawyer I interviewed suggest that people who commit violent crimes and homicides be free from consequences. To the contrary, the lawyers I interviewed generally recognize there needs to be some consequences—they are just generally opposed to executions. For instance, Brenda Telles talked about how she does feel terribly on behalf of families of those who have been murdered and even understands that some people do need to be removed from society even if she does empathize and care for them.

> Like, you know, if someone has committed a violent crime you know, I get they need to be removed from society until they can live peacefully. I mean I don't want violent people running around the streets, I get the criminal justice system, I advocate on one side but it doesn't mean that you know, I don't understand the purpose of all of it.

Later in her interview, Brenda told me about how she feels towards those who are horribly impacted by the murders committed by her clients.

> …It's very hard because you know, I have enormous sympathy for the families of these crimes. I mean if someone was murdered, usually they are in the cases I get these days, they, they family of the victim is in intense grief, intense anger and pain and so I do sympathize with them and so I, and yet I am still against the death penalty. So I think a lot of people don't think you can have both feelings. Like you must be against them if you're for him and I don't see it that way. I am truly sorry for their loss and for the agony they're going through and whatever they say being angry and hurtful or e it forgiving, I give them permission to say whatever it is they want. They are angry and hurt and I do not judge them at all like however they're dealing with it, they're dealing with it.

Wyatt Desmond had a similar position.

> I got people, I give talks all the time and I think the perception is that tI don't think there should be prisons and that's not true. Do I have clients that I don't think should ever be out again? Yes, but that's rare. Do I think people are so institutionalized that they spend so much time in prison that they can' live out here? Yeah. I'm not part of that's not their fault – it's not _all_ their fault- …Not, I'm not condoning their actions, and people, I think people confuse, victims included…but people often times I think prosecutors and especially victims think that our representation is somehow condoning the acts of the client. Nothing could be further from the truth. I have complete empathy and sympathy for victims. But that's not my job. I have a duty and loyalty to one person and that's the person sitting beside me. And I believe so much in the constitution and I think the death penalty is such a political, politically motivated, unfair process that it just has to go. Otherwise we wouldn't have

over 300 guys walking off death row, most of them from DNA testing that they didn't do.

Not every lawyer I interviewed talked about having empathy with victims or society even when prompted. Typically though I got the impression that they did care because they often used adjectives to describe the murders their clients committed as "horrible," "awful" and "brutal." Although not said out loud, they understand the pain and suffering that victims and the surviving family members feel. Nonetheless, no matter how much empathy and sorrow any of the lawyers feel towards victims and others impacted by horrible, awful and brutal homicides, it will never get the vast majority of these lawyers to ever support the death penalty because of a moral anger towards the practice of state sanctioned executions.

Moral Anger Towards the Death Penalty

Robin Steinberg wrote that a primary reason he has been working vigorously as a public defender for over 30 years is that he _hates_ unfairness; unfairness from his perspective pervades the entire criminal processing system.[16] The operative word in Steinberg's position is 'hate.' Steinberg's sentiments can be seen not just as a hatred towards unfairness but more broadly injustice. Witnessing injustices is likely to invoke feelings of anger.[17]

Overwhelmingly, the attorneys I interviewed spoke of executions, as a method of punishment, with a deep moral outrage and sense of anger. For instance, Lewis Frankfurter told me the following:

I have a deep personal commitment to do what I could to fight against the death penalty. And I felt that the way I could do it is one case at a time, one client at a time…So you take those cases because you think the government is

---

[16] Steinberg, Robin (2013: 182–183). "Fair Play." In: Abbe Smith & Monroe H. Freedman (eds) *How Can You Represent Those People?* Palgrave Macmillan: New York, NY.
[17] Horberg, Elizabeth (2011).

doing something that's legally and morally wrong and you want to be part of standing up against that and defending someone.

Similarly, Frank Powell stated the following about the death penalty when I asked why he ever took a death penalty case and continued to defend them after his first:

I believe philosophically, morally, every which way, I mean it's an abomination…The commitment to fighting has never wavered. When you're asked to step up to the plate on something that important, that's what you do.

Morality is only part of the issue—Louis Frankfurter, like so many of the lawyers I interviewed discussed the anger he feels when doing death penalty cases. Sometimes, that anger is directed at more than just the death penalty itself but how it is engaged with by third parties.

It invokes quite a bit of anger that is difficult to control…Invokes a lot of anger at the media and at the public at large who really doesn't understand the criminal justice system but is so quick to pass judgments and takes sides in high profile cases and so I get angry at that sometimes. The media is, the media believes, from what I've seen, the media appears to believe that their rights and their first amendment privileges trump everything. Fourth amendment, fifth amendment, sixth amendment area ll second tier to their first amendment right to broadcast everything. I've seen them go against court orders, I think that they way in which they portray all cases, as they play out, all criminal cases, is irresponsible and it does a lot of harm.

That said, when the interviewees discussed anger, it was primarily directed at the use of capital punishment and those who chose to seek death sentences. Anger though is not only why the participants keep fighting to save their client's life—as the interviews will indicate it also sustains them emotionally so they can keep litigating when new capital cases are brought by prosecutors.

In his interview, Darrell Kappers encapsulated his anger and hatred toward the death penalty by condemning the practice from a moral perspective.

> *I never thought the system was fair and equitable; in fact, I've always thought it to be an atrocity…For me it is visceral. I cannot get pst the fact that they are gonna drag a guy down the hall and stick a needle in his arm and kill him like a fucking dog. That is just morally wrong…fundamentally, it is an argument of decency and morality.*

Similarly, Brenda Telles told me about her level of resentment towards the death penalty:

> *"You know, when people say 'do you like this job?' I think to myself, no, I don't like it. I don't like it because I don't like the death penalty, I despise the death penalty. So I have time and again offered to turn in my law license and go do something completely different if they would get rid of the death penalty. So I don't like it, I don't think it should exist, so I should not have to defend against it. I hate it. But it's there and people are charged and facing it and I just sort of find myself drawn to fighting against it, I mean I can't resist the fight as much as I hate it…I am philosophically, morally, emotionally, physically opposed to the death penalty so it angers me every time I have a case."*
> Interviewer: *"And is that what sort of drives you to keep going?"*
> *"I suppose. Yes. It's the anger. It's the you know, I don't think they should have to, it is my opposition to it that motivates me to fight this hard and to sacrifice what I do to fight it…there is a lot of human emotion going on, I just do not allow the prosecution or government to decide who gets to live and die. I mean you can be, I understand their emotional part of it but I don't understand the you know, making it a law that you get to decide whether someone lives or dies."*

In similar fashion, William Duggan talked about his moral outrage and anger towards the death penalty as a method of punishment.

> *I hate the death penalty. I feel a moral obligation to fight…and my moral outrage…I just can't stomach it…And that's what it comes down to.*

While moral anger towards the death penalty as a method of punishment is prominent among the lawyers I interviewed, morality was not the only reason to hate capital punishment. For instance, Larry Dunn made it very clear where his anger towards the death penalty is rooted in more than just moral anger.

> *"It's (the death penalty) wrong, I don't care if one person is in favor or a billion are in favor, it is wrong and that is my motivation...arguing that a human being should not be strapped to a table and killed is the correct position morally, ethically, spiritually..."*
>
> *Interviewer: "So what is your opinion on this idea that social science is basically kicked out of death penalty litigation?"*
>
> *"Oh, you're talking about McKlesky v. Kemp.[18] That case is a blight on American jurisprudence that ranks right up there with Dredd Scott[19] and Korimatsu.[20] Dredd Scott returns runaway saves to slavery, Korimatsu imprisons American Citizens because of their race and ancestry and McKlesky says yeah even though you're black and you kill a white and are four more times likely to get the death penalty, well, close enough for government work. It is a blight on American jurisprudence but it allows you as a defense attorney, you have to show your decision makers are motivated by race in your case then fine lets have a hearing...to get your ass off this case because you're a racist and I can prove it. You want me to prove you're a racist? Fine, I'll prove you're a racist. Not too many judges want to go through that."*

Of all the lawyers I interviewed, only Christopher Nelson said he was not morally opposed to capital punishment but did tell me that in his opinion the death penalty does not serve any legitimate purpose such as deterrence and as such should probably go away as a form of punishment. Nelson told me that in the end, he is motivated to do a good job and fight hard for his clients because that is the job and what is required by the constitution. In respect to the constitution's guarantee of competent representation, Christopher Nelson is not alone—almost every lawyer I interviewed talked about their duty as an attorney. While highly respected—nobody doubted his skill as an attorney—it seemed that Nelson was a bit of an outsider in the death penalty defense community in Colorado and his interview showed that while he may not embody a moral opposition to capital punishment it does not mean

---

[18] 481 U.S. 279 (1987).
[19] 60 U.S. 393 (1857).
[20] 323 U.S. 214 (1944).

one cannot be an effective death penalty defense lawyer. Nevertheless, as a cultural attribute, it certainly appears that those embracing a culture of resistance possess a deep moral opposition to the death penalty as a method of punishment.

Conclusion

In his book *The Science of Evil*, Simon Baron-Cohen brings forward a debate about appropriate punishments for people who have killed.[21] On one hand, there is a belief that when a person takes a life they essentially forfeit remaining rights to their own existence whether it be life in prison or an execution.[22] On the other hand, there comes a time when a person has spent enough time in prison (i.e., paid a fair price) for committing a homicide that they should be let out to try and enjoy some freedom with their remaining years.[23] Baron-Cohen's position is essentially the same as the attorneys I interviewed when he stated: "…I am against the death penalty. It is not just barbaric (and ironically makes the state as un-empathetic as the person it seeks to punish), but it closes down the possibility of change or development within the individual. We know there is already evidence that components of empathy such as emotion recognition can be learned.[24]" Baron-Cohen's point seems to be that brutal punishments such as the death penalty say far more about us as people inflicting rather than those who receive punishment. In other words, those actually implementing the death penalty may be no better than those being executed. The death penalty lawyers I interviewed certainly seem to embody this perspective in that they can empathize with the anger and pain from the victims and family in regard to the loss of a loved one—the empathy ends with the actual implementation with the death penalty.

---

[21] Baron-Cohen, Simon (2011: 181–184). *The Science of Evil: On Empathy and the Origins of Cruelty*. Basic Books: New York.
[22] Id.
[23] Id.
[24] Id., at 184.

For the death penalty defense lawyers, where empathy ends anger begins. The anger is reserved for the death penalty and its implementation. In this chapter, I focused primarily on the anger the death penalty defense lawyers feel towards capital punishment as a practice. In the next chapter, I focus on the people anger and resentment is reserved for—namely judges and prosecutors and how this ire shapes the legal arena of a courtroom where narratives of life over death from a culture of resistance are presented.

5

Active Resistance—Creating Ideological Boundaries and the Fight Within

In Chapter 4, I argue that prosecutors and judges are part of a dominant group in capital litigation while death penalty defense lawyers and their clients belong to the subordinate group. It is the moral anger towards capital punishment and empathy felt by the death penalty defense lawyers that provide the emotional basis to engage in resistance to capital punishment. This chapter is dedicated to showing what acts of resistance look like during the interactions between judges, prosecutors and death penalty defense lawyers.

As discussed in the introduction, culture is the product of relational interactions between groups that are influenced by their various social, political and economic experiences mediated by the exercise of power of dominant groups through dialectic forms. With capital cases, death penalty defense lawyers argue to have their client's life spared within an arena that is hostile to such a cause because the entire process is activated and managed by a dominant group that is presumptively in favor of executions. It is through these dialectic processes in the courtroom where the resistance culture comes to life.

The resistance culture in the courtroom is mediated through two processes: (1) ideological separation between the death penalty defense lawyers, judges and prosecutors and (2) financial support provided to capital defenders. Ideologically, the death penalty defense lawyers see judges largely as unfair partisans biased in favor of prosecutors as opposed to neutral arbitrators. Further, the death penalty defense lawyers see prosecutors as cruel, dishonest, judgmental and unprofessional actors. This ideological separation is essentially the boundaries that justify aggressive litigation strategies. As for resources the death penalty defense lawyers discuss being given enough financial support to conduct meaningful investigations and conduct aggressive litigation strategies—this money mostly comes from the state government. This chapter ends by discussing how the aggressive litigation strategies look and feel in practice.

Judges

In theory, judges in Colorado are supposed to be unbiased and unprejudiced as commanded by the code of conduct.[1] There are constant claims of judges being biased against lawyers and clients that come up in all forms of litigation—especially in the context of capital punishment. However, unless a defense attorney is in possession of actual evidence of bias against them or their clients then the claims will go nowhere. The lawyers I interviewed by and large felt the judges are in fact biased and prejudiced in favor of prosecutors to help them win a guilty verdict and secure a death sentence. However, the views expressed varied in intensity. While some of the participants were seemingly hostile in their views towards judges, others were willing to say that the biases exist but it varies from judge to judge. In other words, some judges are seen as not being too bad and trying to act in a manner that is not so easily perceived as biased towards prosecutors. Nevertheless, the perception that judges are in general biased towards the prosecutors is a constant theme expressed among the lawyers.

During his interview, Charles Park stated that he feels that *"judges don't really allow for trials where the defendant truly gets a fair shake. I think they*

---

[1] Colorado Code of Judicial Conduct 2.3 (A).

fold to public pressure and allow themselves to be pushed around by prosecutors." William Duggan stated "*The judges are usually prosecutors…they're all the same guy. The judges are the prosecutor. They were the prosecutor, they think like prosecutors.*" Duggan, who secured multiple life sentences over his years defending death penalty cases later in the interview stated "*I mean judges love to blame me, the defense attorney, for everything that goes wrong.*" In other words—he felt that judges would blame him when a case did not end in death which is an expression of their bias in favor of prosecutors and their goal of executing a defendant.

Larry Dunn expressed the same "prosecutor in a black robe" mentality of William Duggan and also indicated that in their rulings judges will hardly ever side with him no matter how good his arguments are when I talked with him about his approach to death penalty litigation—a topic I'll expand on more later in this chapter: "*…If you go in thinking, well we've got some great legal issues here, the prosecutor in the black robe is fully prepared to deal with your great legal issues by fucking you straight up the ass with your great legal issues. If you think you're gonna win on that, good luck, you are not.*" Clarice Montez told me that from her perspective, she felt that the judges by and large are biased against her and defendants in all criminal cases—not just death penalty litigation.

> "*…the judges seem to be uh, annoyed at the amount of work that we do and the amount of work that we're forcing them to do. Um, my impression is for the most part that they want to get this shit over with, uh, um, they'll, you know, uh, periodically lose it with me and start yelling at me about, you know, what I'm doing. I mean that's something that I am used to, you know occasionally judges will yell at you and I'm used to the yelling,* **I think there's a high frustration level about the length of time it takes to give someone due process. Uh, you know, there's the inevitable ruleing [in favor] of the District Attorneyss**. *I don't think that's necessarily a change from regular criminal defense to death penalty work.*"

Montez like Dunn just seems to expect the judge will rule against her no matter what which is one reason for her perception that judges are biased and thereby unfair. Furthermore, Montez's statements about being yelled at because she feels that the judges just want the cases over with and to not do so much work—an issue I'll discuss later in this chapter—is an indication that she believes judges want expedient trials and eventual death sentences at the expense of defendant's receiving a fully fair trial where their due process rights are honored as guaranteed by the 14th amendment. More simply, Montez appears to feel that judges want quick and efficient trials despite the high stakes inherent to death penalty litigation and due process rights be damned.

Wyatt Desmond's feelings, which mirror Duggan, Dun and Montez's, really emphasized the political nature of bias and unfairness coming from judges. Here is how Desmond responded when I asked him why he feels judges are not fair and biased towards the defense in death penalty cases:

> "…Because they [judges] are all gubernatorial appointees too. Go look at the number of defense lawyers that have been appointed to the bench in the state versus prosecutors."
> Interviewer: "…do you, I mean do you feel that in all the cases you've worked on judges have actually been pretty fair with both sides?"
> "No, because no, I don't think judges are fair. Judges. I'm going to use [REDACTED] case again. Because I, the outrage after the [REDACTED] life verdict, the judge that gave life got death threats. There were editorials taken out about how the judge, you know, should be kicked off the bench. There was a private businessman down there who's not even a fucking citizen, he's a Canadian, who at the beginning of the case offered one of our lawyers money to get off the case. Would pay him if he would turn down a public defender job, pay hm money if he would turn down the case. The reams of editors, of letters to the editor, the television reports, and yet when it came time for us to try our case on the heels of that with three [COUNTY REDACTED] judges, we couldn't get a change of venue, even though juror after juror after juror came in and said they read about, heard about the case, talked about the case with family, saying these guys should be you know, castrated, hung, and then burned. Could not get it moved to a different jurisdiction. Judges would not move it. Do I think we were getting a fair shot? No."

During our conversation, Desmond went on to tell me about a specific incident where his feelings and perceptions of unfairness and biases from judges were validated:

5 Active Resistance—Creating Ideological Boundaries ...

"They would give us the opportunity to litigate our motions. There was never, never were we given an opportunity to boot them [judges] off the case. In the [REDACTED] case the trial, judge [REDACTED] who's retired, we got a change of venue and that was because the prosecutor asked for it…I think the [REDACTED] case was ridiculously unfair. We had judge [REDACTED], took that case over for us. He was not being fair at all. He was one of the judges that sat on the [REDACTED] case, he is one of the judges that voted for death and there was, there's a glitch that we found in the court rules around death penalty jurists and what it said is because when we were doing 3 judge panels, what it said was basically 'these cases are so hard that no judge has to sit on more than one a year. And we hated our judge and he was going to do the [REDACTED] case and he had already noted for death in the [REDACTED] case. And so we filed a motion to kick him off citing both his verdict and the fact that judicial rules said you can't sit on another one. He was outraged. I don't know if he talked to judicial lawyers or what, but he came back, got on the bench and said he was going to recuse himself. We haven't had a trial yet, we've had a year of motions before the recusal and as he's getting off the bench in a packed courtroom where we're gong to have to try the case he says with all the media there "I would have given him death too." And bangs his gavel and walks out of the courtroom. That sound fair to you?"

It certainly seems that in Desmond's mindset, the judge should have known the rules of sitting on more than one death penalty case a year and recused himself long before filing motions for such relief. Furthermore, it was bad enough that the judge puts it out to the media and community members that he would have given the death penalty in a case where they have not had a trial or been allowed to put on mitigation. What really makes things worse for Desmond is that the statement "*I would have given him death*" which indicates that the judge 'predetermined' a death sentence in apparent violation of numerous rules in cases such as *Morgan v. Illinois*[2] stating death sentences that are pre-determined before hearing any aggravating or mitigating factors during the sentencing phase of a trial violates the 14th amendment.

---

[2] 504 U.S. 719 (1992).

Desmond's point is that how can anyone get a fair trial or have their pre-trial motions adjudicated and considered in a fair and unbiased manner when one of the judges overseeing the trial had already made up their mind to decide in favor of the prosecution's request for a death sentence? Fairness seems to be nothing more than judges giving the defense attorneys an opportunity to file motions and litigate them knowing that in all likelihood everything will be decided in favor of the prosecutors no matter what the law actually says. His point is well taken and certainly supports the perception that judges are not inherently fair or unbiased.

Death orientated judges were a major concern for some of the participants and a primary reason they believed judges were biased and unfair towards them and defendants facing possible execution. Ricky Donaldson had a similar viewpoint as Wyatt Desmond in regard to judicial bias in favor of a death sentence:

"I mean, the particular judge we were in front of was death penalty orientated it seemed to me; and prosecution orientated. Not you know, so he was creating air but just so it was a pain in the ass and you we are fighting an uphill battle at every point."

Donaldson's perspective is that the different levels of scrutiny and resistance from the judges are an outward manifestation of unfairness and bias in favor of prosecutors. Frank Powell said in his interview he did not want to talk in too much detail about his cases which was respected. Nevertheless, I still asked about how he perceived judges and if they were being fair during the litigation. Frank stated the following:

"Well, I don't think [judges] favor the prosecution more in death penalty cases more than they do normally. I think they favor the prosecution generally… The prosecution in the eyes of most everybody is the good guy and we're the bad guy. The judges know if they err on the side of helping out the prosecution too much that some appellate court will reverse it and it'll come back down and there will be another trial. Whereas if they err too much on the side of the defense and it gets found not-guilty well the prosecution has no remedy. So I think that judges have sort of a natural and philosophical, and to a certain extent understandable, sense that it's better to err on the side of the

prosecution than it is on the side of the defense. But in the death penalty cases I was involved in, it wasn't any worse than usual."

Powell, like the others already discussed, perceived the bias and unfairness against defendants by judges generally like Montez. However, Powell's statements indicate that there is a political component—namely that overall it's just better to err on the side of the prosecution because if they are too defense heavy, they will hurt the prosecutor's chances of a victory which appears to be a political calculation as highlighted by Darrell Kappers

"Well honestly, I think most judges are patsies of prosecutors. There are a lot of judges I have respect for but I've noted a very dangerous trend in the judiciary especially in certain, more traditionally conservative, jurisdictions. Prosecutors seem to be bringing more political pressure on judges to limit the judges discretion. For instance, if a judge starts to make a decision that the prosecutors office doesn't like they will create a file for them; they will investigate them; they will create transcripts of hearings and trials with them; they will start to release snippets to the media about them...There is a judge named Judge [REDACTED] and w wasn't a defense orientated judge by any stretch but more fair considering the jurisdiction and the prosecutor didn't like him so they start applying all this pressure on him, political pressure, make statements to the media and get on this stupid fucking radio show and run their mouth about these activist judges making their own law and that kind of crap and eventually he was accused of being a racist and he couldn't take it so he said 'screw this I don't need it I'm going back to my law practice – I don't need to be called out by this lunatic prosecutors office so he eventually stepped down.' It feels like there is a fear of this happening with judges so there is more and more...".

The biases and unfairness the participants feel exist and come from (a) prosecutors and judges essentially being one in the same person (i.e., a prosecutor in a black robe), (b) more interested in expedient litigation over honoring due process requirements under the Constitution, (3) pro-death penalty orientated and (4) political motivations. That said, a number of participants talked about how they feel biases and unfairness exist but leave a little space that at least some judges, but not all, do try and be fair and remain unbiased.

In my interview with Peter Reynolds, he told me about two interactions with judges in separate death penalty cases that led him to believe unfairness and bias against defendants exists in the death penalty.

> *"So the relationship with the judge was really, really bad. Jury instructions, I mean, crap, he [judge] didn't want to tell the jurors that he [the client] was going to be in prison for the rest of his life.*[3] *The judge thought somehow or another it was something they didn't need to know when making their decision on life or death but to the point where we're sitting in this room and we're arguing…I mean I finally, and its not the way to act, literally, I threw down my pencil, it bounced about eight feet in the air and I stormed out of the courtroom and [REDACTED] came out and got me back and we went back in and we ended up getting the instruction."*
>
> Interviewer: *"Did you feel that he was at least being fair despite the rocky relationship?"*
>
> *"I thought he was really unfair many, many, many, many times. But you know, I thought about it a lot since, and sat down and talked to him [the judge] a few times since…and I think he was probably doing the best he could. I think he was struggling the best he could."*

However, while Peter Reynolds was willing to acknowledge that the judge he was dealing with, after conversation, maybe wasn't intentionally unfair as initially perceived it did not mean he believed judges were always acting in good faith. In the second death penalty case, Peter told me about the sentencing phase of a death penalty case, when 3 judges were on a panel and making decisions of life or death instead of a jury. When the sentence was handed down—a life sentence albeit—Peter felt that the two of the judges who voted for death were motivated purely by political calculations in order to avoid social scrutiny.

> *"So there were two judges from [COUNTY-A] and one from [COUNTY-B]…One of the two [COUNTY-A] judges would have gone life but when they found out the guy from [COUNTY-B] was going to go life, they pulled*

---

[3] By law jurors are to be told that a life without parole sentence instead of death means a defendant will never leave prison.

back and went ahead and voted death so it was two to one. It still had to be unanimous for death and as a result, the guy from [COUNTY-B], I mean the guys from [COUNTY-A] didn't have to stand up to their community and tell them why they made that choice, and the guy in [COUNTY-B] took all kinds of heat because, it wasn't his town but he took all kinds of heat. He had aspirations of being on the court of appeals and that was just gone. He had, I mean, it was god awful. It was just, you know, it was emotional and it was political and it was all media driven and it makes you be a little angry about that stuff."*

Similarly, Tina Carlson and Carl Reese told me about how they feel and perceive that judges can be, and have been fair in their cases, but that it is not a universal truth.

"I think that judges, in general, favor prosecutors yes. In the last one that I did, here, Judge [REDACTED], well we didn't actually take the case to trial but I think he did a really good job. Judge [REDACTED] in the [REDACTED] case, I think he tried to do the right thing…but other judges in general I would say no. I think they are, I don't think they enjoy doing death penalty cases, I don't think any judge wants to do them. It is, I think, incredibly hard on the judges."

"You know, although I didn't agree with certain rulings, it was, I felt the judge was very fair. I mean I definitely didn't get a sense of any bias on their behalf."

Interviewer: *"So you would disagree then in your case there was a prosecutor in a black robe mentality?"*

"Yes, yeah. And I mean even in other cases I've been involved with, I see some, the whole system is somewhat biased against the criminal defendant. I mean that's just the reality, if you read appellate cases, I mean the whole system is to a great extent biased against criminal defendants. It's sort of the, you know, other than our sort of constitutional protections, there is, there's a huge weight of authority and everything else against the defendant, but I mean, you know, for the most part in the cases I've handled, I've felt the judges that I've dealt with were dealing with tough situations as best they can. Although I might not agree with their rulings. And I know some of my brethren would radically disagree with that assessment. I've also seen other judges, in other cases that I haven't had to deal with that were I'd say no, I mean they're the worst of the worst and I don't, I think they're badly motivated and everything

else, but I haven't had to deal with that in the cases I've handled that were death or potential death cases."

Tina Carlson and Carl Reese did not specifically tell me why or why not they felt a judge was being unfair or biased against their clients—again it is a generalized standing perception.

That said, while there is a perception that judges are unfair to the death penalty defense lawyers and their clients two of the attorneys indicated the general perspective of judicial bias can be overcome. Lewis Frankfurter and Brenda Telles, when I asked about their feelings and perceptions about judicial fairness, talked about how judges can be perceived as fair. In his interview, Frankfurter stated:

> "I've had good judges, good experience with judges who have struggled to apply the law in a fair way. I've had very good judges. It's been a good experience with them…**in terms of the law**, I've had really good judges. No hint of unfairness or biases towards my clients, even in the worst cases."

Frankfurter makes a specific point about why he doesn't feel the judges were unfair or unbiased against him—it is 'in terms of the law.' This statement indicates that as far as Frankfurter is concerned when judges are allowing him to litigate his case and are not operating outside of the law, from his view anyway, then they are not being biased or unfair. This is essentially what Carl Reese was describing when he stated simply disagreeing with a judge's ruling does not mean they are inherently being unfair. In like manner, Brenda Telles told me that she found, in her experience, that when judges would let her litigate cases fully as required by law fairness was then achieved but she did not expect much more from any judge.

> "I will say that the judges in part, because I think they're made to under the law, they don't shut us down too much on our mitigation. Mitigation is what saves our clients lives and its anything we say it is and they seem to go along with that. So I appreciate that they let us present our mitigation and then they, **I have not run into a judge who has shut me down on doing what I wanted to do in defense of my client**…In one trial I was not shut down in picking the jury which is also important; it was seven weeks and it made

me mentally ill but he let me go for as long as I could stand it to get the jury I wanted and in the end that worked out, so they have given us, me at least, what I needed to do to do a good job. **Now leading up to that, you know, I have not experienced much extraordinary courage on behalf o the bench, I have not come up against someone who was going to stray from the mainstream of judging these cases, I've not thought 'wow that was really courageous and right and just and you know, I've not been extremely impressed**. I've simply been allowed to do that which the law absolutely positively says I have the right to do."

Interviewer: "…other participants have this viewpoint of the judge as just a prosecutor in a black robe but you don't seem to really have that."

"It depends, I mean I've been in front of a number of judges and you know, some literally were prosecutors and some literally prosecuted death penalty cases and now they are the judge, so obviously they identify more with the prosecution and give leeway to the prosecution. I don't think I've ever been in front of a judge who defended a capital case. Ever…There are those who have defended death penalty cases and have become judges but I have not been in front of those people."

Like Frankfurter, Telles is indicating that from the defense attorney's perspective, a judge's fairness seems to be a function of them allowing the death penalty defense lawyers to litigate their cases in a manner allowed by law even though a judge is probably biased in favor of the prosecution. In other words, judges can behave fairly but they will never be completely fair. Brenda Telles' statement that she is 'going up against' judges and that they tend to give prosecutors leeway is an indication that judges are at some level still biased toward the prosecutors even if they let her litigate the case. As an example, in her interview, Brenda Telles told me about an incident where a prosecutor likely violated a court order right in front of her and the judge, during a death penalty trial. Despite the apparent violation, the judge did nothing to determine if a rule or court order really was violated and whether or not appropriate sanctions against the prosecutor should be applied.

"I had an expert and the expert writes a report. And you know, you always ask the judge, you have to in capital cases, if there's reciprocal discovery unlike regular cases, so in death penalty cases I have to give them stuff, the prosecution stuff that I wouldn't have to give them if it were a DUI or a noncapital murder, which seems strange, but I have to give them stuff that I get. And so when we do that we're always asking the judge to redact things out of there that may not be relevant or for whatever reason to redact it and in this one experts report, the judge said 'yes, I will redact one sentence' and so he takes a sharpie and this is before trial, crosses out the sentence he redacts, copies it, gives it to the prosecution, that's your copy. My expert is testifying at trial, has his report on the stand, the prosecutor is questioning the expert and says 'may I approach' and the judge says yes. And it dawns on me why he's, or why I think he's approaching, and I say judge we need to approach the bench right now, can we please approach the bench now? In the meantime the prosecution goes to the stand, asks the expert to see his report, reads the sentence on the clean copy, puts it down, I am so outraged at the bench, I'm like causing a scene, I tell the judge what my suspicion is, the judge says to the DA 'why in the world did you need to approach the witness at that point and see his report?' And he said 'oh, it just seemed like the font of his report was different than the font of mine so I was just checking to see if the font was the same.' And I know 100% why he approached, that he read the redacted sentence on the clean copy, and he did that knowing he shouldn't do that. I believe that 100%."

Interviewer: "Was there any consequence for the prosecutor?"
"No."
Interviewer: "Did that, for lack of a better term, piss you off?"
"Yes."
Interviewer: "Is there anything you can even do?"
"No, I mean, by that time, they've been a district attorney that long, you know, they don't make rookie mistakes or they don't do things, there will never be a point where they say 'oh yeah I approached the bench to look.' It will always be 'I was looking at the font.' And I mean, you can try and do things and I certainly have made the complaint for the sake of making the complaint but not because I've ever seen anything done."

Generally, the death penalty defense lawyers seem to believe that judges are, or at least can be, biased against the lawyers defending a person facing possible execution which increases the likelihood of receiving a death sentence. That said, the amount of bias judges have in favor of prosecutors is likely to vary from jurisdiction to jurisdiction.

Rita Townsend who does appellate work in Oklahoma and Colorado told me the following about judicial biases in her work:

> "*In Oklahoma, they're horrible, they're just horrible. They're so pro-prosecution, they're so dismissive of the defendants, jury selection in Oklahoma would be enough to make you scream, it's so bad and so biased. Um, in Colorado I think it's less obvious, I think the judges in Colorado at least are in my experience are trying to be fair and to be methodical and um, they're trying to get it right. They don't often or always succeed, but I feel like the Colorado judges, um, take the death penalty very seriously. Oklahoma, it's just I don't know, it's very different. They're very um, they're trying to do things quickly and they're very nasty to the defense lawyers. Not all judges, there's a couple of judges that I've seen in Oklahoma that are a little bit better.*"

All in all, the perceptions of death penalty defense lawyers broadly suggest they see judges as an adversary that can be relatively fair but are nonetheless partisans. The lack of judicial fairness then is the ideological boundary between death penalty defense lawyers and judges.

Prosecutors

While some of the participants were willing to make room for the possibility that judges are at least 'trying their best' similar feelings were rarely granted for prosecutors. This makes sense—it is the prosecutors that decide to seek a death sentence, not the judge. The initial decision to bring a capital punishment case—a method of punishment all but one participant is opposed to—understandably causes most of the death penalty defense lawyers to view prosecutors more negatively. The negativity in large part comes from the inability to empathize with the prosecutors decision to seek death. For example, Ricky Donaldson stated:

> "*I remember thinking, 'how could you,' I mean you as a prosecutor, I never said this out loud but, 'how can you try to execute somebody?' 'How can you like get your mind in a place where that seems like the right thing to do under whatever circumstances?'*"

Larry Frankfurter told me that the decision to seek capital punishment caused him to lose respect for prosecutors:

> "…And I think I lost respect for some of them and I haven't had much experience along these lines, but for some of them who felt that the end justifies the means, I have't seen many of those but they're there. They're out there. And I really disrespect them a lot. I have no respect for that."

Finally, Larry Dunn, in response to the question "how do you sleep at night knowing you're defending guilty people?" told me he feels that type of question is best suited for prosecutors in death penalty cases:

> "…well really you should ask prosecutors that question, I mean how can you spend your education and your skill and experience and your time on earth doing everything you can possibly do to strap a helpless person to a table, stick a needle in their arm and inject poison into the until they are dead? How do they sleep at night? That is the question you should be asking prosecutors?"

In the previous chapter, I demonstrated that the death penalty defense lawyers empathize with clients and the families/victims of the murders committed by the people they are trying to spare from execution. However, as also discussed in the prior chapter, the participants are staunchly opposed to the death penalty and as such just cannot really understand the reasoning prosecutors have forever trying to execute another person no matter how vicious the underlying murder.

It is this inability to understand the reasons for bringing a capital case that causes death penalty defense lawyers to largely view everything about prosecutors and their behavior in litigation pejoratively. Brenda Telles told me the following when speaking about prosecutors:

> "You know, I cognitively understand their job. I have always said I could never do their job and I really you know, I'm okay with prosecutors until they start cheating or doing things I don't like where they're unfairly judgmental. So I mean if they present the facts that they have, you know, and do it in that way, then I understand their job and I understand the role that they play. But you know, when they get to what I feel to be unfairly judgmental or you know playing fast and loose and stuff like that then I'm not a big fan."

In the section on trial strategy, I'll demonstrate how these views about prosecutors, and to a lesser extent judges, influence the approaches the defense lawyers take in fighting capital punishment and thereby giving life to a culture of resistance. For the time being, I want to keep the discussion on the impressions and feelings the participants have about prosecutors who bring and fight to secure death sentences because it is the inability to empathize with prosecutors decision to seek a death sentence and thereby frame them in a generally negative perspective that creates a clear ideological boundary between the government narrative of death and the defense lawyers who respond with overt acts of resistance. To be more direct, the inability, or more likely unwillingness, to empathize with the reasoning a prosecutor has in bringing a death penalty case is an ideological boundary that delineates sides within a legal culture of resistance.

To begin, Brenda Telles' interview provides a general sense into how most of the participants in this study viewed prosecutors. Thematically speaking the majority of the attorneys I interviewed described their impressions of prosecutors who seek the death penalty with a variety of constructs such as (a) unfairly judgmental, (b) politically opportunistic, (c) dishonest, (d) cruel and (e) unprofessional. In the previous chapter, I talked about how the death penalty defense lawyers are all opposed to capital punishment and for all but one they express a deep hatred toward the practice of executions. That hatred in many ways transfers to prosecutors since they are the ones deciding to seek the death penalty and it heavily informs each death penalty defense lawyer in how they approach the task of defending a person from possible execution by the government.

During his interview, Wyatt Desmond told me a ton about his perspective on prosecutors and their conduct during death penalty litigation when talking about how he interacts with opposing attorneys.

> Interviewer: "…is that your experience, that you actually work hand in hand with prosecutors, you're cooperative and move forward in that type-of manner?"
>
> "No."
>
> Interviewer: "Is it very contentious?"

"Very contentious."

Interviewer: "How so?"

"It's contentious in the motions practice, it's contentious in the litigation, it's contentious in even trying to have negotiation discussions. I have a very difficult time sitting across the table from someone that wants to kill another human being and have a nice discussion. What motivates them to have the contentious? I think it's right or wrong, they (prosecutors) believe they're on the moral high ground. I think it's political. I think they're extremely judgmental and I think they have to spend a lot of time with an outraged victim that puts them in a box where they may want to do something but won't…do we have to talk? Yes. Does it get to the point where sometimes you can't talk? Yes. The [REDACTED] case is a good example. I came onto it late, William Duggan had been litigating it for a long time. He and the chief prosecutor couldn't speak anymore. I got permission to go take a run at trying to deal the case one more time. I did and I was told because of what Duggan has done (being contentious with prosecutors), there will be no more plea offers in our life-time - and then we got forty-seven not guilty verdicts - they could have had life!"

Interviewer: "What did Duggan even do to get them so angry?"

"Litigated the case. William is one of the best lawyers I've ever seen and certainly one of the top capital litigators in the country. And he did what he was supposed to do. He litigated the case. They (prosecutors) don't like litigation, they want it to be easy. Judges don't want it to be hard…"

Here, Wyatt makes it clear that he sees the relationship between prosecutors and defense attorneys as contentious rather than cooperative. This contentiousness stems from a number of considerations such as prosecutors being described as believing they are morally superior in their decision to pursue capital punishment when instead they are seen as judgmental and political. Later in the discussion, I asked Wyatt Desmond about why he thinks prosecutors pursue capital punishment and he told me a specific incident with a prosecutor:

> "I'll tell you what a prosecutor told me when I was doing [REDACTED]. When I was litigating the case he told me he had seen so much death in Vietnam it just didn't matter to him anymore. I think that's a pretty callous way to look at an individual that you're trying to put to death."

> Interviewer: "Do you think most prosecutors have that sort of view point?"
>
> "No, I don't know, I can't answer that. I can't. I don't know what motivates prosecutors. What I do know is that we have pockets of death penalty worlds in this state. We don't have death penalties across the state, we have pockets. And it seems to be in the more (politically) conservative jurisdictions. Significantly more religious jurisdictions."
>
> Interviewer: "Does it ever bother you, the whole thou shalt not kill thing?"
>
> "Yeah, I don't understand that. I don't understand how you can carry the entire bible around on your iPad and yet believe that, I'm not a real religious guy, I believe in something, but if I'm going to believe in something, it's the new testament, no the old testament. I thought the whole idea about Jesus coming down here; they've never seemed to get, they don't seem to be able to get out of the old testament and yet they're still bible thumpers. I don't understand that. I don't have the capacity to understand how you can be pro-life until that baby grows up and does something bad and then you're pro-death."

These last quotes from Desmond demonstrate that he not only sees prosecutors as being judgmental and political but also cruel and contradictory.

Carl Reese generally agreed that the death penalty being sought by prosecutors was politically motivated.

> "I think that politics plays such a crazy role in the entire criminal justice system because we have this sort of fear based mentality and it's a combination fo the actual effect of the political process of sort of fear-mongering tough on crime mentality, you know…Politics plays a role in the fact that we even have the damn death penalty because it's such a fear mongering issue that they use the absolute exception to the rule about why we should have this utmost penalty. But we could see that pendulum is swinging back on that. So politics plays a role all the way up to the district attorneys making decisions. I think district attorneys are primarily political animals, you know, so they may have their signs on higher things. They may honestly believe it. But the politics and political forces are significant in pushing for, having the death penalty as a penalty and in pushing the prosecution to seek it in certain cases."

The tough on crime political mindset bothered a number of the lawyers. Tina Carlson revealed a deep sense of hatred and disgust for prosecutors seeking what she saw as excessive punishments and when they pursued the death penalty for what may only be political purposes:

> "*I had trouble being a hater before I did a death penalty case. I think that I started become a hater with the chronic offender program. I mean, the death penalty is a huge issue to me, but also a huge issue to me is the life sentences and don't get me started on sex offender sentencing laws right now, they're, it's barbaric and Draconian. And the chronic offender program and how it was used, yeah, no, that was when it, and I also, had the experience of representing five kids charged as adults in murder cases and one fo them is still doing life without parole. And he was sixteen...right before the trial his mother fired us and he got an attorney, bad, ineffective assistance of counsel in my opinion, and was convicted of first degree murder when he was probably not, he was only guilty of vehicular homicide.[4] He drank at sixteen years old, drove and hi a kid. And he's doing, he was doing life...In hindsight the sis kind of, I never ever got over that because I believed this kid was doing a life sentence and was not guilty of first degree murder and I never let go and I wrote [THE GOVERNOR] a letter and he got, when he left office he commuted his sentence. That's the good news, he commuted it to thirty-two, making him parole eligible. He's been in prison now, he's thirty-six, so he' seen in prison twenty years now. So, then the District Attorney [REDACTED], who was the special prosecutor in the case got angry at [THE GOVERNOR] for doing that so he, when we went to the parole hearing, he was denied so he's still in prison, so I'm working on still trying to get him out, but, the District Attorney [REDACTED] was on TV on the news a couple nights ago and my husband who doesn't really have anything to do with my world here, he saw a different side of me, I mean, **all of a sudden I saw him, I said, you know, I mean, the hate that I have for that man (The District Attorney) just spewed and it's very different from how I am in general** but my husband was, 'whoa,' and I said that's the man who is responsible for this kid and that was racist, it was a racist prosecution, the kid, it was the kid that got hit was white and the defendant is a sixteen year old gang banger and he was, they made it into a gang case when it wasn't. It was a drunk driving case and yeah, **I probably the bigger issue of anything for me personally has been what we do to kids who kill. I hate it, I hate it...I just cannot*

---

[4] Vehicular homicide statute: What is the penalty range.

understand how a person can attempt to put a kid away for the rest of his life. His brain isn't even developed, so, I have issues. Anger issues."

Interviewer: "Was death penalty litigation then very contentious?"

"Yes, very contentious."

Interviewer: "And did that spew into the personal relationships?"

"I can honestly say that in [REDACTED]'s case the prosecutor [REDACTED], when I first got to [REDACTED], he even told once that he didn't believe in the data penalty and [REDACTED] is a unique jurisdiction because it's democrats and there are people in the District Attorney's office who actually don't believe in the death penalty unlike down here or [REDACTED] where everyone does. And then when he got on the case, it affected it because I felt like he lied. And he was doing a [REDACTED] move, saying I personally don't believe in the death penalty, but It's my job to do it and he worked so hard to try and kill [REDACTED], it did affect my relationship with him…he's just a tool. He was not very real, he was just like a robot."

For Tina, the implementing of what she sees as harsh and unnecessary punishments is manifest cruelty but to do so even when the prosecutor does not believe in the utility of the punishment, such as an execution, they are more than just tools and robots; they are dishonest. Clarice Montez did not expressly say that she hated prosecutors or found them to be 'tools' or 'robots' but nevertheless did not speak in a way that indicates she them as being unprofessional:

Interviewer: "During litigation what are your opinions on, your experiences with prosecutors…?"

"Vitriolic, vitriolic is really the best way. Um, I really have never, I mean I was a trial lawyer for twenty years before I started doing death penalty cases and never in my life have I experienced such unprofessionalism and vitriol from the other side. Um, just sarcasm, rudeness, just really strange."

Keeping in line with the general theme, Clarice is demonstrating that not only does she see prosecutors as unprofessional but also cruel and judgmental with her statements about prosecutorial vitriol. Frank Powell had a similar sentiment as Clarice and told me the following in his interview:

> "*None of the cases I was involved in was there a breach of professional ethics on part of the prosecutor of the sorts you sometimes read about...That said, I think that, I saw prosecutors regularly behave in a fashion that I would call somewhat unprofessional even if it's not unethical....Their (prosecutors) goal is supposed to be justice, not a conviction and I think that some prosecutors lose sight of that goal, no matter what kind of case it is. It is particularly egregious if they lose sight of that goal, the goal of justice, when it's a capital case and when it becomes, you know, I'm gonna win this case as opposed to I'm gonna see that justice is done.*"

Here, Frank feels that when prosecutors only strive to win their case (i.e., send a defendant to prison so they will be executed by the state) and disregard all other considerations they are then being unprofessional. Certainly, some prosecutors and judges would disagree with Frank and claim that an execution of a defendant who killed one or more people is justice. Setting aside the debate about what is or is not justice, Frank's perspective is fairly straight forward—the job of a prosecutor is to do justice and capital punishment is not justice. Thus, by not trying to do justice, the prosecutor is behaving unprofessionally.

In a similar vein, Darrell Kappers told me that he sees some prosecutor's behavior as "…devious, slimy, unethical and criminal…I do not use those words lightly." When I asked Darrell to expand on his perspective on prosecutors, he told me the following:

> "*Yeah, prosecutors lie man, they lie all the time about things going on. When it reaches the death penalty level it becomes a very personal thing for them…they end up losing all professionalism about it and there is no exercise of professional judgment about it and it all becomes a win at all costs game no matter what you have to do. That is then the perception that this guy (defendant) is so bad we (the prosecutors) need to kill him and do whatever we have to do to kill him whether it be lie, cheat, steal, coerce or manipulate anyone we have to so we make sure we win and ill this buy because is is just so bad.*"

William Duggan expressed similar viewpoints in his interview:

> "*I still teach the bigger the case, the more they (prosecutors) are going to cheat. In a death penalty case, you know, they get so freaked out that any chink in*

the presentation of the evidence is going to result in reasonable doubt or a lessening of the resolve of one juror to give death right. So they freak out and hide or manipulate the evidence or sometimes the cops do it and they (prosecutors) cover up for the cops. But I found misconduct in every case, I don't know why they do it. You have to ask them. Why they're driven to do that is beyond me. I just look for it."

Peter Reynolds told me about his feelings and perspectives on prosecutors specific to when they engage in 'cheating':

"Fuck, fucking pisses me off that they'll cheat in that context. I mean, I don't like cheating anyways…I came into the the public defender system thinking…I thought the cops were sort of full of shit and were sort of the establishment…and I've learned that one, I was right. There are a lot of lying cops. There are a lot of good cops, really a lot of them who I think are trying really hard to do a good job and they'd lose the case before they'd lie and it puts them in context of being human but you take a case to a death penalty case? I mean its bad enough if you're going to put somebody in prison over lies, but a death penalty case? It happens. And prosecutors who like play cheating, bull shit games in a death penalty case. I mean, I just don't, it's unacceptable. I mean it's outrageous and it should never, ever, ever happen. And it does. I absolutely despite the two people who were the primary people who were [prosecuting] cases and this case against [REDACTED], I just. Yeah."

Later in his interview, Peter told me about a situation where prosecutors were 'playing games' and as such being in his perspective cruel and unprofessional:

"…They (prosecutors) play games, you know? [REDACTED] had this case in [REDACTED] and as part of trying to convince the prosecutor not to seek the death penalty, brought in the defendant's mom for a meeting at the prosecutors office…the U.S. attorney over here was trying that case. And so the mom came in and among other things fell on her knees in front of the prosecutor, crying and saying you know, 'please don't do this, please don't seek the death penalty, I know he's done bad things, I know he's made this mistake and you know, I know he's done bad things and I know he's this and that,' you know, negative things and well they sought the death penalty. You know, I don't hold any particular anger over them seeking the death penalty just

because this guys mom got down on her knees in front of them, I mean, in this world that's simply not going to happen. But, they call her as a witness during the death stage. They endorsed her and put her on the witness stand because of the negative things she said about her son during that plea, to try and kill the motherfucker. They didn't get it (a death sentence) but to try it. Ow, you tell me, is that somebody to hate or not? You know, it's a God awful thing to do...And fortunately he (the prosecutor) got to eat his own shorts on it, very publicly. But you know, I mean, there's lots of reasons to be distrustful of the other side in these cases and so, yeah, yes, anger toward the prosecutor? Sure."

The cruelty of a prosecutor, as Peter sees it, comes from their willingness to use a mother's pleas in a private setting to try and see her son's life—albeit not keep him out of prison on a life sentence—and force her to testify in a way that could end up leading to her son's execution. Finally, Rita Townsend told me about her views on prosecutors throughout the litigation process as being unfair and cruel:

"No, no I don't think they (prosecutors) are fair at all. I think it bothers me greatly when I see how eager they are to, just how bloodthirsty they are and their zeal for the death penalty and how they want to try to lie, cheat and steal their way to get it. Um, I see that more in Oklahoma but it happens in Colorado too and um, I mean, my, my disgust about prosecutors in general is that I think a prosecutors job is to represent the people and to serve justice and not to win at all costs and what I see I practice is prosecutors who are so hell bent on winning that they will do anything to get there and I, that's wrong. I think prosecutors should always be conceding valid points and that should be their role. If the defense has a valid point it should be conceded, they shouldn't be fighting just for the sake of fighting right? That's, they're not, they're not the same as an ordinary litigate, the Supreme Court's told us that many times..."

Overall, the majority of death penalty defense lawyers see prosecutors unfairly judgmental, unprofessional, dishonest, cruel and politically opportunistic. However, Christopher Nelson, the former prosecutor who is regarded as one of the best death penalty defense lawyers in the nation had the following to say about how most death penalty defense lawyers view prosecutors:

"…I recognize that, um, people's beliefs and their behaviors are influenced by forces beyond their control. That uh, the way you were raised impacts how you think. Um, an dum, that helps me to understand my clients and the people who are facing the death penalty. Now a lot of members of the defense community that do capital cases get that. They get that their clients, for whatever reason, were impacted by forces that turned them into the people they are and because of that, they are forgiving or they find it mitigating. But they're unable, or unwilling, to display the same grace to prosecutors that they are to their client. You know, prosecutors believe the way they believe because of the way they were raised. There were influences in their lives that turned them into who they are. It doesn't make them evil people. It means they have a difference of opinion, but there's too many defense attorneys who treat prosecutors as if they're evil. They're not. They disagree wit you. I, I do not like the way a lot of capital defense attorneys practice law."

Interviewer: "Would you mind elaborating a little bit on that?"

"They practice, they, they, they think that anything goes, that because their cause is right, because their cause is just, they feel at liberty to do whatever they please and pursue that cause. To be dishonest, to be unethical. And I don't."

Interviewer: "If you don't mind, I mean, do you have any particular experiences of the dishonesty, unethical behavior, by the actual capital defense attorneys?"

"Yeah, but I'm not going to share them."

Interviewer: "Okay, that's fine."

"And you know, prosecutors, prosecutors sometimes are dishonest too and unethical."

Interviewer: "From everything I'm learning through this project, the high stakes of what's going on tend to get to people."

"I think that's right, I think the high stakes of what's going on causes people to lose their perspective and their judgment."

Christopher Nelson's viewpoint is important because he is acknowledging, like the other participants, that prosecutors can at least be unethical and dishonest but are far less willing to believe they are cruel or overly judgmental. Nelson's viewpoint also provides a great segway into the next section on how death penalty lawyers tend to litigate their cases. The participants generally recognize that death penalty defense litigation is 'high stakes' and requires an incredible amount of hard work. It will be up to readers to put a moral, normative, framework on the trial strategies as alluded to by Christopher Nelson.

Adequacy of Resources

Death penalty litigation is very expensive. On average, a death penalty trial in Colorado costs between $2 million and $3.5 million according to the ACLU of Colorado.[5] The prosecution of James Holmes cost over $5 million <u>before</u> the trial even began.[6] Since most of the death penalty defense cases are handled by the Colorado Public Defender's office, it is the responsibility of the state to pay for the costs associated with death penalty defenses litigation. When the public defenders office does not take a death penalty case, Colorado has some cases taken by private defense attorneys that are appointed through and funded by the Colorado Alternate Defense Counsel ("OADC"). In Colorado, if a public defender cannot be used, the Colorado Alternate Defense Counsel appoints experienced private lawyers[7] and pays them $85 an hour plus all necessary costs to conduct a proper defense (OADC, 2013: 8). This rate is much lower than private lawyers funded through the Criminal Justice Act—a federal program similar to the OADC—which are paid $175 an hour and costs to defend death penalty cases.

By and large Colorado funds death penalty defense lawyers much better than what is seen in other states. Steven Bright documents a multitude of cases outside of Colorado where death penalty defense lawyers were paid an hourly rate ranging from $11.84 to $20 per hour and

---

[5] McKinley, Carol (2015). Aurora Theater Shooting Case Costs Colorado $4.5 Million—and Counting. http://www.westword.com/news/aurora-theater-shooting-case-cost-colorado-45-million-and-counting-7446825.

[6] Sickles, Jason (2015). Cost of Colorado Theater Shooting Case Exceeds $5 Million Months Before Opening Statements. https://www.yahoo.com/news/cost-of-colorado-theater-shooting-exceeds-5-million-months-before-opening-arguments-185259025.html.

[7] Capital defense attorneys in the Alternate Defense Counsel must have a minimum of 10 years of prior full time criminal defense experience in order to be allowed to defend a death penalty case (OADC, 2013).

denied funding for expert testimony, office staff and the like.[8] Richard Deiter of the death penalty information center provides data demonstrating how little some lawyers get paid for defending a death penalty case. For example, Kentucky lawyers in private practice are provided $5,000 per case. It is estimated by experts having years of experience in death penalty litigation that to properly defend a capital case a lawyer should put in a minimum of 1,000 hours of work. The math is easy; Kentucky death penalty lawyers—if they do the job properly—will make around $5 per hour. In Philadelphia, Common Pleas Court Judge Benjamin Lerner ordered a study investigating the compensation scheme for private sector capital defense lawyers in Philadelphia. The study showed lead counsel is paid a flat fee of $2,000 to prepare a capital case, including the first half-day of trial; for the rest of the trial, a lawyer gets $200 for half days and $400 for full days.

During the interviews, I asked participants about their approach to defending death penalty cases. One of the issues I inquired about which would have implications on their strategy is whether or not they were provided enough resources by the state and court to adequately defend a capital case. Each participant agreed that the prosecutors had more resources at their disposal but in the end, felt that they had enough to fight and win their cases. I asked William Duggan, one of the most highly respected death penalty lawyers not just in Colorado but across the nation about adequate resources and he told me the following:

> *"Yeah, we had adequate resources. We didn't have, well you know, we don't have a built in core of liars, you know, called the cops right? You know, which will try and turn themselves into experts on anything you know? 'Look in his eye, I could tell by the look in his eye that he was, you know, this or that. These guys, you know…or the guys that always remember the statement they never wrote down, you know? I love those guys. 'Oh, my guy just told me out in the hallway that you guys said this,' 'oh, really?' 'Did you ever think for a minute he's a fucking liar?' 'No no no no no.' And then the judges have to make, then the exception to the discovery rule is the exception to the sequestration rule. You know, just busting out the exceptions. Then they (prosecutors) go into*

---

[8] Bright, Steven (1994). Counsel for the Poor: The Death Sentence Not for the Worst Crime but for the Worst Lawyer. *Yale Law Journal*, 103: 1835–1883.

private practice as a defense lawyer and they wonder why they suck. Because, you know, there's really no work for out of work prosecutors."

Duggan's point is that while he may have had the resources necessary to defend a death penalty case, the prosecution always had more whether it be the favoritism of judges granting 'exceptions' in order to bring what is perceived as inadmissible expert evidence into court or having a biased police force on hand that has already conducted an investigation and brought in expert witnesses.

Of course, not everybody I talked with expressed such intensely negative views of the police while acknowledging they were provided adequate resources and support in order to defend death penalty cases. Carl Reese told me the following about his experiences in regard to being provided resources from the state:

Interviewer: "…did you ever feel like you were sort of outgunned by the prosecution?"

"No, no. Not in Colorado. Colorado's very good about providing significant support for the defense of death penalty cases, so have never run into a situation where we felt outgunned. I mean you know in the [REDACTED] case we had some of the premiere experts in the state and in the nation. I mean they were national experts. So no, have not felt outgunned. They're (prosecutors) clearly able to bring a massive amount of resources against you but in Colorado, frankly, we do pretty well in terms of providing the resources to do defense cases. I couldn't imagine doing it in some other states."

Peter Reynolds had a similar perspective:

Interviewer: "So then resource wise when you were doing this [death penalty litigation] did you feel like you all at the public defender's office had adequate resources?"

"Yeah, I mean I thought we had resources. I mean, we travelled all over the country, we traveled where we needed to travel, saw what we needed to, did it multiple times. Good investigators, we would bring out witnesses when we needed to, you know. Had decent experts. Yeah, I felt we did."

Larry Dunn expanded a bit more on the sentiments of Peter Reynolds and Carl Reese when talking about having 'caps' on resources available to the defense. Typically, the state of Colorado would reserve a set amount of money that is allocated to the defense for use in hiring investigators, experts and the like for litigation purposes. However, Dunn told me that the state would 'loosen' those restrictions so that the financial caps were never really enforced.

> "*If you're in private practice and have a firm and making the $80 an hour on a death penalty case which is what the state of Colorado pays you cannot keep your doors open and support associate attorneys and paralegals or anything like that. So it is definitely a money drain.*"
>
> Interviewer: "*So resources wise do prosecutors have an advantage?*"
>
> "*Well in a lot of states for sure. In Alabama they still have severe caps on capital representation. Colorado they don't necessarily enforce the caps and I mean states are loosening up much more than they used to but clearly prosecutors have an economic advantage when prosecuting a death penalty case over the defense in terms of all the ability to mobilize resources.*"

Dunn's point is well taken given the information I provided above in regard to Kentucky and Philadelphia. However, Colorado as a state has gone out of its way to provide resources for death penalty defense lawyers so they can litigate their cases fully.

Not everyone necessarily agreed that they had adequate resources when put in comparison to what was available to the prosecutors. For instance, Lewis Frankfurter stated the following when I asked him about the amount of resources, he was provided as a private practitioner doing death penalty cases:

> Interviewer: "*…Did you feel that you were on par with what the prosecutors had or did you feel like you were undermanned?*"
>
> "*I felt that the government, I believe that 5th government always has greater resources, I think that's a fact of life. They always do. I don't think any judge, state or federal, in my death penalty lawyering, has ever denied me anything that I needed. And the reason is, because if they knew if I came to them and asked for it, that I needed it, that I was serious about tit, that I knew what I was doing and I wasn't wasting money, that I wasn't trying to*

spend money just to wear everybody down or to be antagonistic and if I asked for it, I needed it. And they gave it to me, without fail, Every one of them, every time."

Interviewer: "OK"

"I had one judge who had no idea what he was doing, had no, shouldn't even be a judge. Had no idea what he was doing. And purported to deny me an important resource and the DA found out about it and came over and stepped in and said, 'You're wrong. He's entitled to this. And he's entitled to it confidentially.' And I got it. That judge wasn't on the case very long, but for him, it was just a lack of knowledge. He didn't know what he was doing. The other judges who know what they're doing, when I would come to them and ask for a resource, I've never been turned away...I had what I needed. I mean, I think they (prosecutors) just inherently have greater resources."

Darrell Kappers, like Lewis Frankfurter had a similar sentiment in regard to resources but felt that bringing multiple death penalty cases caused significant strain on other lawyers especially when the defenses are being handled by the public defenders office. Specifically, Darrell Kappers stated the following when I asked him about having resources:

Interviewer: "During the trials do you feel that you had adequate resources as compared to prosecutors?"

No, not at all. I never had a problem getting money to do stuff if I needed to go somewhere and interview witnesses or like the brain scan on [REDACTED]; they all got paid for and psych experts and never arguments in that sense. Were we understaffed? Certainly and we have made efforts to change that. [REDACTED] and I have been able to hire paralegal sand social workers to do mitigation. Doing [REDACTED] I had a second chair named [REDACTED] and she is very smart and hard working along with [REDACTED] and [REDACTED] the investigator and there is a lot for 4 people; in fact impossible for only 4 people....I've tried to build more resources into the capital unit but when you got more than 1 case you have to juggle cases and spread resources around and decide staffing and it is not like you can go out and hire a lawyer to do this. You go to work on a death case you have to give your other cases to someone else and you cannot just go hire a new person. It is always difficult to shuffle resources around.

The point being made is that while the courts would give public defenders and private attorneys enough money to hire experts and conduct investigations, they were still understaffed from a labor perspective. Within the public defender's office, the strain coming from doing multiple death penalty defense cases was clever—lawyers trying those cases not were being allocated more funds and what little labor power was available at the expense of the remaining cases. Public defenders are already overworked—death penalty cases ensure that not only will they lose workers to just one case but also all of their tasks and responsibilities need to be assumed by an organization that cannot go out and hire replacement workers—even if only temporarily. Nevertheless, the overall perspective is that the state of Colorado did ensure that by and large death penalty defense lawyers had adequate financial resources to conduct a full defense.

Aggressive Litigation Strategies: An Overview

Having adequate resources gives the death penalty defense lawyers the legitimate ability to fight incredibly hard to save their client's life. During the interviews, I asked the participants about how they litigate death penalty cases. While the personal style and demeanor of the attorneys vary, there is uniformity in two respects. First, the attorneys all focus on putting mitigation packages together in order to keep a case from actually going to trial and a plea for a life without the possibility of parole (LWOP) punishment can be reached. Second, if a case does go to trial, the attorneys embrace an aggressive trial strategy in order to either win during the guilt/innocence phase of capital punishment litigation and the punishment phase where a jury determines if a defendant will or will not be executed. Overall, the approach the lawyers take is a complete rejection of the 'courtroom workgroup' construct previously discussed.

My interview with William Duggan who may consider responsible (and praised) for creating the structure of death penalty defense litigation in Colorado highlights the complete process the attorneys take when they begin defending a death penalty case. Duggan told me that he focuses first on doing a heavy mitigation investigation to try and convince prosecutors not to pursue capital punishment. However, once prosecutors decide to take a case to trial and secure a death sentence Duggan, and all of the others, engage in very aggressive litigation to defend their clients and secure a LWOP sentence.

> *Interviewer: "Basically, what was the strategy?"*
> *"I mean, we would approach them and we'd do a heavy investigation. We'd start our mitigation package because the basic strategy is this; is you've to this guy who's usually done a pretty high provide crazy thing, OK? Because the death penalty is pretty much reserved for really mentally ill people because mentally ill people do crimes on a huge scale. You know, just ugly crazy stuff you know?…And they usually have a root cause of a reason why this exists right? So what you do is get on it and you move a lot of resources to you know litigation in terms of understanding the factual crime and understanding the mitigable crime."*

If the prosecutors are not receptive to the mitigation package, then the process of aggressive litigation begins. When discussing how he litigates cases, Duggan told me the following:

> *"You litigate heavily every little piece of evidence and law OK. So mainly what the strategy for us at the time was we would come on if they were really serous about death and it looked like a deather and smelled like a deather…we'd bring in a team, appellate lawyer, parter up with local lawyers and you know it was just gonna be if you wanna stay on the death case sentence it's gonna be a machine. We're just going to litigate everything. You know, we're not, it's not part of the local get along gang. We're just, you know, and if we catch you lying or cheating we're going to turn you in and report you, I mean it's just no holds bar litigation. Every legal issue, every factual issue, any mistake…We're playing for your jobs OK? You're playing for our clients life, we're playing for your jobs."*
> *Interviewer: "So it's no cooperation with the DA?"*
> *"You know what they can do? Stop pursuing death. But, so at the same time I'm trying to convince them I'm going to beat you, it's gonna cost a lot of money, you're going to put a lot of political capital out there and if you don't get death then you look weak and ineffective right…so beat 'em, save my clients life, just beat 'em. I'm not going to stipulate to anything, I won't*

5 Active Resistance—Creating Ideological Boundaries …

stipulate to anything. You know, it's not the get along school. We're not going to get together, go over motions and agree on this, nothing. Zero."

Interviewer: *"So it's an anti-workgroup mentality then?"*

"Yeah, we're not a workgroup. Not a workgroup. No, you know that's the persona we had to put out you know…We're going to be strict constitutional lawyers. Litigating every issue. File 455 motions. And they'd always say, you know, 'you're filing all these motions Duggan.' You know they actually took juries away from us for a while, you know and screwed that all up because they couldn't beat us. So I'm like, well you know, find one that's, you know, all these, what they call them, you know, I forget its some kind of a motion where the claim is you filed something that didn't have value. So, why don't you (prosecutor) pick them out and grieve me for them? Not a one, because you can't. Because we really knew what we were doing. I mean, you know, they just whine about it. Whine, whine whine."

Interviewer: *"How would you describe the way you were, you would carry yourself in court."*

"I don't take shit."

Duggan's interview indicates that built within his litigation strategy is the politicization of the death penalty. As the following quote, it has a purpose during the entire process of defending death penalty cases:

"…you know, we're politicizing the death penalty because the death penalty is not a judicial issue, its not a justice issue. The death penalty is a political issue. So you deal with a political issue as a political issue. You know, they would try to make, you know, the whammy is that if they use a defense attorney to actually go along with their bullshit that the death penalty is a justice issue, it's not. It's a political issue. So we tried it on a political plane…We didn't get the same money, we politicized it, you know? You know, we say that they're doing it only to you know, they're killing black men who kill white women because they're racist. That's the kind of stuff we say."

The goal by politicizing the death penalty was to try and convince prosecutors not to pursue capital punishment and accept a LOWP plea based upon the mitigation package presented. If prosecutors feel that there is enough mitigation available to convince a jury to give a LWOP sentence instead of death then the argument is it will be a massive political mistake by the prosecutor to pursue a sentence they know is unlikely to be delivered. As such, the prosecutor then risks losing social standing within their office, potentially might be fired for spending so much time and money on a case they knew would not likely end in a death sentence and maybe forfeit career advancement outside of the prosecutors office because the loss will be very public. Later in the interview, Duggan gave me an analogy about how he saw himself and his role generally in death penalty defense work:

> *"…So we don't try to do shit, we just do shit you know. I mean…conceptually I would think OK well everybody is on a trampoline. The judge is bouncing and the DA is bouncing and they want me to bounce at the same tempo right? Well, I've got to figure out a way to stop and pop right? That's literally what you do, so, otherwise (the client) is gonna just bounce you right along to the old gas chamber. So you don't become that guy. You don't become the helpful 'Judge, oh I've got that for you. Oh judge, can I help out? Oh judge, I'll waive taking that record, no the court reporter doesn't need to be there for that, judge. Oh no, it's all good with me.' You can't be that guy."*

Overall, Duggan's approach was substantially similar to the strategies of other lawyers. The initial goal is to put a mitigation package together in order to convince the district attorney to accept an LWOP plea and forgo pursuing capital punishment. If the district attorney decided to seek death, then the lawyers fought tooth and nail in order to make the process of securing a death sentence incredibly difficult and increasingly unlikely. As the record shows, by and large, the death penalty defense lawyers in Colorado were incredibly successful in securing LWOP sentences for their clients and avoiding executions by following the pattern of (1) start putting a mitigation package together and (2) litigate cases aggressively until a life without parole sentence is secured either in plea negotiations or from a jury.

Mitigation

Larry Dunn, who is one of the most widely recognized death penalty defense lawyers in the country did not mince words when he talked about his approach to death penalty litigation. Larry's approach recognizes that in the end, like all of the other lawyers I interviewed, need to work within a system they find to be unfair and stacked against them so when he is in litigation the strategy is always on how to win over a jury deliberating between giving a death or LWOP sentence.

> *"You know once you learn the rules of the game you function within the game and I mean you know…corruption…it is really not that different…Cops lie all the time on the witness stand. Once you realize that, and once you realize the judges are pretending to believe these lies although nobody in the courtroom believes them, the prosecutors put on this big show and testimony, judges pretend to believe it and that brings us to the saving grace of juries. I mean, it is a corrupt system but it is corrupt everywhere and like I tell young lawyers once you begin to understand there are two prosecutors in every single case and one of them is wearing a black robe you can inevitably function within the game."*

The point of focusing on juries, for Dunn, is that jurors are the most likely to be honest which is a rarity in what he perceives as a corrupted system.

> *"…the one thing that still surprises me after thirty-one years is that I am still constantly surprised by the corruption of judges and the dishonesty of prosecutors."*
> Interviewer: *"How do you get around it?"*
> *"You don't, I mean it is what it is and you just deal with it. The saving grace in the system is the jury. What separates this country from say Iran is that in this country we have juries. Juries are honest and juries __will almost always do the right thing__ and that is the only thing that separates this country from China or Iran in its judicial system."*

Dunn's faith in juries only goes so far and for good reason in death penalty litigation. The reality is that years of empirical evidence have demonstrated that (1) the decision to seek death by prosecutors and (2) the choice to give a death sentence instead of LWOP from juries is highly biased against racial minorities—particularly black men. The judiciary through decisions such as *McKlesky v. Kemp* has done everything possible to ignore these empirical realities and make it virtually impossible for people facing a death sentence to have it converted to LWOP or be granted a new trial because the original death sentence is based upon the racial biases of jurors, judges and prosecutors.

Nevertheless, as the preceding discussion sections have argued the entire death penalty process is administered in a manner that is highly disadvantageous to the defense and favorable to a death sentence being achieved. Hence, the importance each and every lawyer puts on the process of building a mitigation package—it is this information given to prosecutors prior to a trial and juries during sentencing that is used by the defense lawyers to try and secure a LWOP sentence. If prosecutors are unwilling to accept a plea to a life sentence, then the defense needs to ensure it has a strong enough mitigation package ready to go for a possible sentencing hearing if the defendant is found guilty of murder. The strength and depth of the mitigation package can often be the difference between a client getting a death sentence or life in prison.

Building a mitigation package is no small matter. Some of the attorneys talked to me about the lengths they would go in order to create a mitigation package compelling enough to convince prosecutors to accept a LWOP sentence instead of pursuing death; failing that—to convince a jury that LWOP is the just punishment. Carl Reese told me in his interview about a massive mitigation investigation he did to keep a death penalty case from actually going to trial.

"*...it becomes all consuming...the preparation was enormous. Lots of trips out of town to meet with people.*"

Interviewer: "*Would you mind telling me more about [the case]?*"

"*Yeah. [REDACTED] grew up in [REDACTED]. We went out, met his family, did, found out a lot of, you know, got a lot of medical records, school records and once you started to put together the picture again it's like, my god, this guy had a massive shitty childhood, there was just no way around* it. Evidence of many, many, early emergency visits that were highly suspicious. Suspicious explanations for those. We got to work with some very interesting folks who were sort of top experts in their field. Our psychiatrist [REDACTED] who has actually written with, I forget the name of our neurologist, had written on sort of causes of murder, we got to work closely with brain scientists, there was a guy [REDACTED] we got to work with who had done studies on frontal lobe damage and had shown the difference between the brains of murderers who were much more planned as opposed to murderers whose crimes seemed more spontaneous and there tended to be evidence of frontal lobe damage in the more spontaneous people. The frontal lobe, pre-frontal lobes tend to act as the governor one human behavior, controlling the more primordial impulses and you know, fairly established that frontal lobe damage could be a problem…Just learned a massive amount."

Although this case Carl Reese worked on did go to trial, it ended in an LWOP decision instead of death. What is demonstrated though is how much front end work goes into putting a mitigation package together. The underlying homicide in Carl Reese's case involved breaking into the home of a young woman and brutally raping and then murdering her. The point of all the mitigation Carl Reese collected was to show that the crimes, which are without question horrible, were the result of serious mental disability, nothing was planned but instead, this all happened on impulse and that there was no 'enjoyment' by the defendant. In other words, Carl created a mitigation package that stated the defendant should not be sentenced to die because the crime resulted from serious brain damage and was not done for some personal pleasure. This argument, backed up by significant evidence, was enough to secure LWOP.

Lewis Frankfurter told me that all of this mitigation work is important because in the end, they are trying to get past what prosecutors call 'the abuse excuse' defense lawyers bring forward to convince juries that people committing murder deserve to have their lives spared.

"…the prosecutors coined the term 'abuse excuse' several years ago and they'll say 'this is noting more than the abuse excuse, you know, we've all had or known someone who had it just as bad or worse and who became a doctor or a minister' and so it's hard defense to run. Everyone's on the family history

> *and you have to investigate the family history; you have to show it and you have to present it…the ones you win are the family history where the person was actually physically hurt and caused mental issues, was actually physically hurt in some way which resulted in cognitive loss…and those are the cases where you can show an MRI."*

Overall, the mitigation package is a necessary component to a culture of resistance because it represents a manifest an identifiable attempt on behalf of death penalty defense attorneys to counter the government's narrative that people facing capital punishment are the most vile and unforgivable individuals on the planet and therefore need to die. Doing such a deep dive into each client's history and current mental health status serves as a basis to refute the state's characterization of each client by showing the crimes are explainable as opposed to justifiable while humanizing the client and giving juries a reason to show mercy. None of this is an easy task and requires significant time commitments, sacrifice and skill by legal professionals along with adequate resourcing. When done correctly, the mitigation package has the ability to be so powerful in resisting the state's characterizations and reasoning for the death penalty that they change course. However, when the mitigation package does not work on prosecutors then the fight moves into a courtroom and death penalty defense lawyers begin focusing their efforts on litigation.

Litigation

Death penalty trials have two phases—a guilt phase and a sentencing phase. In the guilt phase, it is up to the prosecution to persuade a jury that the client is guilty of capital murder. The second phase of a death penalty case is sentencing which occurs if a client is indeed found guilty of capital murder. The goal of this section is not to provide an overview of the strategic components of litigation. Rather, I hope to describe the intensity these lawyers bring to the courtroom in order to stop their client from being executed by the state of Colorado. The intensity these lawyers bring is incredibly uncommon in typical county and district criminal courts and completely rejects conceptualizations of courtroom culture such as 'workgroups' or 'managerial systems[9]' where judges, prosecutors and defense lawyers are certainly oppositional but rarely if ever engage in overt acts of resistance.

Throughout the interviews, each of the participants indicated to me that more often than not death penalty cases involve clients who are without question guilty. Nevertheless, it does not stop these lawyers from pursuing a not-guilty verdict—sometimes they get acquittals. Hence the importance of being aggressive during the litigation process. For example, William Duggan, who above I quoted as rejecting any form of cooperation with the district attorneys seeking capital punishment, told me about the underlying mindset he brings to litigation against prosecutors.

> *"We're playing for your jobs, ok? You're playing for our client's life, we're playing for your job…I'm trying to convince them I'm going to beat you, it's gonna cost a lot of money, you're going to put a lot of political capital out there and if you don't get death then you look weak and ineffective right?"*

Duggan was not just stroking his own ego. I was able to confirm he has secured more than one not-guilty verdict in death penalty defense work. These acquittals are important not just for the client but it send a message to other prosecutors that death penalty defense lawyers that embody a culture of resistance are more than capable of getting a not-guilty verdict in a case where everybody believes the client is guilty.

> *"What kind of a big nut guy are you saying you're going to go get the death penalty and you come home with nothing, you know? And what's really great is when you get them acquitted, ok? Because I've even done that more than once."*

---

[9] See generally: Feeley, Malcolm (1992). *The Process Is the Punishment: Handling Cases in a Lower Criminal Court.* Russell Sage Foundation: New York; Kohler-Hausmann, Issa (2019). *Misdemeanorland: Criminal Courts and Social Control in an Age of Broken Windows Policing.* Princeton University Press: Princeton, NJ.

Along the lines of Duggan's approach, Wyatt Desmond talked about stopping a trial to litigate graffiti found on a bathroom stall door that was detrimental to his client.

> "Hell, in the middle of that case we litigated, somebody wrote on the bathroom door in one of the men's restrooms, "[REDAACTED] must die." We litigated who did it, we got the judge to seize the bathroom door and it sat in his freaking chambers for two months. You know, it was inappropriate. The guy that did it confessed. Sent a a ten page letter to the judge or something like that confessing as to why he did it. Prosecutors see it as just smoke, we see it as, what if it was a juror? You know, we don't know who wrote that. What if its one of the cops testifying? How is that not a bias? And the ABA standards for death penalty litigation say you cannot leave, you must leave no stone unturned and we believe in that."
>
> Interviewer: "So you don't really care if prosecutors or judges get angry with you?"
>
> "No, I couldn't care less."

Litigating doors is important and represents manifest behavior that indicates these attorneys are going to fight tooth and nail in rejecting the prosecution's claims of guilt and why a client deserves to die. This willingness to engage in aggressive litigation is demonstrated by Larry Dunn's experience in forcing a trial court judge to remove himself from a case due to racial bias towards a Black defendant. Notably, this was Dunn's very first death penalty defense case.

> "It was a case where a young African American man was alleged to have done a home invasion burglary in the middle of the night of an elderly, white school teacher who was 85 years old and retired and she had one living relative that was her sister; the sister called the next morning and nobody answered and she got concerned and called the police... The police found a broken window, they entered and found her body lying in her bedroom; she had been raped so badly that she had bled out through her vagina and she had been beaten so badly that her face was unrecognizable. My client was found 2 days later driving her car and was arrested in this tiny little rural town in [REDACTED]. They had to move him out of the county jail because they were afraid he was going to be lynched actual–y - this is in the 1980s mind you not the 1880s. They couldn't find any lawyer within 3 counties who would be willing to take the

case so they had to go five counties over to find a lawyer who owed the judge a favor and agreed to do the case for $5,000. The lawyer met the client once for about 20 minutes, plead him guilty straight up to every charge, they went through the penalty phase where no evidence was put on by the defense and the jury sentenced him to death in less than 2 hours. The case was affirmed on appeal by the [REDACTED] state supreme court and then I got the case while a cert petition was pending in the Supreme Court which was denied. I got the case when it went back to the state for a habeas corpus claim."

Although the initial narrative is long, it is important because it helps demonstrate the difference between how Colorado death penalty lawyers approach defendant capital murder cases as compared to other states.

"*Ultimately, we concluded after talking to my client for no more than a half hour that not only is this guy, not only is he seriously mentally ill but also likely mentally retarded as well and the state of [REDACTED] had a mental retardation exemption for the death penalty. We went through a hearing through the state habeas proceeding, lost that and took the appeal to the [REDACTED] state supreme court and…the case was reversed on the grounds of ineffective assistance of counsel at trial.*"

This work by Dunn was only the beginning. After getting his client a new trial, which took about two years, he agreed to serve as the trial counsel.

"*…The trial judge was going to reappoint some hack lawyer who was just going to get this guy sent right back to death row so I step-in and said I would do the trial and the judge then said no I'm not appointing you and so that got litigated out which took forever and the [REDACTED] supreme court eventually said to appoint me so the judge appointed me and I filed a motion to recuse the trial judge on the grounds that he is a racist, that he pulled his kids out of integrate schools, belonged to all white clubs, that he routinely referred to African American defendants as niggers, sentenced African Americans more harshly than whites for the same crimes, that as chief judge of his district in his entire tenure there had never been an African American working the system other than a janitor in counties that just happen to be 40% African American. So we had witnesses lined up for the hearing and right before the hearing he decided you know what just to avoid the* *appearance of unfairness he would get off the case and he then got off the case."*

Getting a judge off of a case is an extreme step for a lawyer to take—especially when alleging racial bias but in death penalty cases a necessary investigation and step considering the realities of racial bias in sentencing practices and deciding who will be charged with capital murder. For Dunn, he was not finished going after people for racial bias.

"...I then told the prosecutor you know, you're next for racial motivated peremptory challenges, for a whole history of of racially motivated preemptory challenges and I will litigate your ass right off this case too. He said lets just wait for the victim's sister to die of old age and we can deal the case and so that is what we did."

Although this was Dunn's first death penalty case in what is a storied career doing civil rights and death penalty defense litigation it demonstrates exactly the type of personality and tenacity required to save a client's life. While getting a life sentence here was important Dunn would get new information about the case sometime later about what was going on behind the scenes before and during the litigation that underscores the need for tenacious practices.

"I get this call from a cop who wants to meet and I said to the guy well lets talk then. He says I cannot talk on the poohs but are you coming back to [REDACTED] anytime soon and I said yeah...So I go down there and I meet with this copy; turns out there are three cops on the police force and he says 'we have no law enforcement authority we basically just do parking tickets and that is it, the authority is with the sheriff. We got to the [murder] scene the same time the Sheriff got to the scene and he would not let us into the house to check things out, he basically just made us stand outside and stand guard but I was taking my shift standing guard and I heard a deputy walk over to the sheriff and heard the deputy say we finally got a warrant on that nigger's house and I heard the sheriff say go get that niggers shoe and we'll fix his ass good.' I knew from reviewing the evidence that a bloody shoe print was one of the pieces of evidence against my client. So a while later the deputy came back with my clients shoe and they go inside; the cop couldn't see

5 Active Resistance—Creating Ideological Boundaries … 113

what happened inside. The cop said that he just wanted me to know about this and I said of course are you willing to testify about all this? The cop just laughs and says to me 'you know there is only one drug dealer in this Sheriff's jurisdiction and there used to be several, now only one, and he has a mansion and a swimming pool and by coincidence the sheriff has a mansion and a swimming pool. There is a reason that these other drug dealers are in prison or are dead.' I found out later there is another deputy on the force who every time he wanted to have sex he would drive out to the black rural part of town and he would literally rape women. One time someone called to complain and the sheriff sent that same deputy out to take the complaint. So of course this cop was not gonna testify for me, no way. He wouldn't sign an affidavit or anything, he just said he wanted me to know the truth about what was going on. So I just said, OK, thanks and that was that. That was my first death penalty case."

Dunn's experience does more than highlight the racial biases inherent in the death penalty but also the cultural and political implications. As stated in the introduction, the death penalty is a local cultural phenomena and thus its use and handling within the legal system will follow culturally accepted practices. Racist communities will have no problem with putting minority individuals on death row—even under very suspect circumstances, appoint local defense lawyers that will not put up a fight and eventually execute the individual that would more likely than not do life in prison had they been white. Local communities that culturally embrace the death penalty are just more likely to use it than other communities which is why over 50% of capital cases happen in just under 1% of all counties across the country. The strategy of saving the life of a client must take the local culture into account. Dunn knew in his case that going to trial would result in a death sentence so he had to find a way to end the litigation early. I asked Dunn about this approach to litigation.

"I guess if you find yourself in a trial everything you've done has failed…when I was just an itty bitty baby lawyer [REDACTED]…says 'Larry, always remember we are in the business of conflict resolution; however in order to resolve conflict there must be conflict." So I have always intuitively known that as a public defender, but another way of saying that is that when you

> clamp down the lid and turn on the heat it is gonna blow, it will blow somewhere and you don't now when it will blow but it will be somewhere and the upshot of that is that it will be a life sentence for your client...in [REDACTED] it was getting the judge off the case...then I've got a prosecutor who doesn't want to go through itigation on the issue of whether you're a racist mother fucker. That is the pressure point. Clamp down and turn up the heat. It has nothing to do with the merits of the case, but that is the blow point and so that is how I approach every death penalty ca–e - where is the blow point, we'll find it, I'm gonna clamp down the lid and turn up the heat."
>
> Interviewer: "So there is no work group stuff..."
>
> "Oh yeah, I know what you're getting at. Fuck that shit man, I will destroy those sons of bitches, I will make their life a living hell and all they are gonna want to do is make me go away and the only way they are gonna make me go away is to give my client a life sentence."

Dunn is not kidding. Later in the interview, he told me about another death row case that had been pending for almost 28 years due to multiple re-trials in a state well known for utilizing the death penalty in very prejudicial manners.

> "...So a disgruntled lawyer in the county ended upending me some campaign literature from the judge presiding in [REDACTED]'s trial where she was touting the fact she cleared the way for the death penalty in [REDACTED]'s last trial so I put together this humongous motion to throw her off the case and we throw her off the case and I then, you know we were the neighborhood bullies. People don't pull this shit in rural county [REDACTED] or [REDACTED] or [REDACTED] or rural anywhere because if they did they will never get another court appointed case for as long as they live. So I throw the judge off the case, that is the pressure point. The DA obtained psych records simply by writing a letter to the prison saying 'give us his psych records,' I then send them a motion saying I think you violated HIPPA which is a possible criminal violation and I'm going to ask the U.S. Department of Justice to look into prosecuting you Mr. DA for a possible HIPPA violation. At this point everyone in the county is in an uproar about the whole deal and we have local counsel who are good ole boys and they are saying to their buddies in town 'hey we got this psycho lawyer from Colorado and we cannot control him, it isn't our fault' and so the prosecutor proposes a deal where the

client gets life. The first condition in the deal is that I have to withdraw. OK, I'll do it. I go down there the day the deal is going down, they are not expecting to see me at the courthouse but I had not formally withdrawn yet and I said 'yeah I'll withdraw I got the papers right here, I just want to see what is going on.' I then file the papers to withdraw and I see a deputy sheriff and he and others literally start chest bumping me right out fo the courthouse saying 'Mr. Dunn you need to leave.' I say to the guy the sis a public courthouse and still they say I need to leave and they are walking –e - chest bumping me out. I think, well my instinct is like fuck you take me to jail I'm not leaving but I know the client needed this deal so I just bit my tongue and I was out of there. That is how these cases roll."

While most of the participants did not go into nearly as much detail as Larry Dunn, the underlying mentality of aggressive and tenacious litigation strategies was by and large made clear. In his interview, Darrell Kappers told me that he intended to send a message about how he would approach trials and why prosecutors should bend to his will rather than the other way around.

"When I got there I started out running and made it clear I was not going to be pushed around…I made it clear early and often I wasn't going to take shit from anyone or rollover…"

Interviewer: "How do you get that message out?"

"Well, just do a lot of jury trials. I would be very frank with people that I think it is a rotten deal, you're being unfair and this is wrong and I won't advise my client to take this piece of crap. It is hard on one personal because it is more work than if you're just some shuck who turns pleas but it develops your practice and reputation…you get a reputation as being willing to fight."

The fighting does not necessarily mean that the lawyers I interviewed were constantly yelling in the courtroom or performing in a bombastic fashion. In fact, most of them from what I gathered during the interviews was that in the courtroom the death penalty attorneys litigated their cases aggressively but tried very hard to keep a professional and dignified tone, tenor and persona in the courtroom and especially in front of juries. The more aggressive language and demeanor during the fight typically take place in motions practice. As Larry Dunn's interview demonstrates, he did major investigations into judges and prosecutors and then the fight moved to what the participants referred to as 'motions practice.' By motions practice, I mean filing pre-trial objections to evidence, challenging of the qualifications of expert witnesses and the like. It takes a very long time to write these motions and even longer to litigate them in court. Brenda Thompson told me about her standard experiences with motions practice in death penalty cases.

> *"In my last case…we did forty full days of motions hearings like sporadically up, leading up to trial. So that would often be weeks, judges tend to set like weeks of motions. In my last case every third week of the month was set off for motions and so you know, you spend a week in court and then you immediately start preparing for the next week coming up and you know, writing the motions, organizing the witnesses, preparing to go to court, dealing with the client, you know, it's all just a constant, you know and some days are worse than others."*

Tina Carlson similarly told me that she spent a lot of time in motions practice when doing a case that was bound for trial.

> *"Motions, motions practice is huge in death penalty work. You are, you would, yeah, you just file motions after motions after motions, we bing up issues after issues, after issues, we call them (prosecutors) on every discovery violation."*
> Interviewer: *"How did the prosecutors respond to it?"*
> *"They had no choice. They have an obligation to file briefs and litigate and whine to the judge about the abuse, it's pretty typical."*

While the vast majority of lawyers engaged in massive amounts of motions practice there were a couple of exceptions but it wasn't for a lack of filing motions—they just did not have the same volume. The best example of this approach came from Lewis Frankfurter when he talked about being more narrowly focused in the motions he brought to court for litigation. During the interview, we talked first about bringing challenges of racial bias which led to a broader discussion of motions practice

5 Active Resistance—Creating Ideological Boundaries …

"*It's a tough fight and its a fight that you're to going to win, but it's worth making a record on (racial bias) in a death penalty case. So I've doe that but I've been I guess I've been fortunate that I haven't been thrust into an environment that I truly felt was personally discriminatory. If I did I would fight it.*"

Interviewer: "*When you're, now with the fight in the courtroom, is, are you talking about challenging every piece of evidence and basically filing every motion you possibly could file on behalf of your client to save their life?*"

"*No, I don't think that it's been my practice to challenge every piece of evidence. If there's a legitimate legal issue, it's challenged, if there isn't its not. I think that in those cases that you have to maintain credibility with the judge and of course with the jury. I think you have to maintain credibility with all the players, the judge, the prosecutor, the jury and I disagree that you should object to every question, you now, fight every piece of evidence that comes. I disagree with that, I think you lose credibility by doing that. You look pretty silly. I think it's that the old story of crying wolf. I agree that it's important to make a record in death penalty cases, laws can change, I certainly, there's always something that the trial lawyer can miss, a case that we didn't see. So I totally agree that it's important to make the record. I think you can do that by filing fifty motions and stand on the motions on twenty-five of them and tell ht judge, 'in this one, we really need a hearing; I'm serious about this one.' And when you do that, the motions that get heard really get listened to.*"

Later, I asked Frankfurter if he felt that his approach could be seen as too cooperative with the district attorneys seeking the death penalty.

"*I don't think it's so much cooperation. I don't think we're cooperating. I think we may be cooperating in the sense that we're complying with discovery rules, we may be coopering in that sense. My school of thought is coopering in the sense that we're not dishonest and we expect the prosecutors to not be dishonest, so I think we're cooperating in that sense, but there's a clear dividing line of, there is clear battle lines drawn in those cases, there's no question. I think that those lawyers who do death penalty cases recognize a clear battle line is drawn and joining the battle full-fledged and yet maintaining some sense of respect and credibility, end up doing so to the benefit of their clients.*"

Conclusion

As this chapter shows, there are (1) clear ideological boundaries being drawn between the judges, prosecutors and death penalty defense lawyers and (2) the legal fight is intense, aggressive and tenacious. From the death penalty defense lawyer perspective, judges and prosecutors are largely one and the same. As such, the boundaries of the arena are clear—it is the death penalty defense lawyer v. judges and prosecutors. While not all of the lawyers interviewed went so far as to say a judge is nothing more than a prosecutor in a black robe nobody ever felt that the judges would do anything extraordinary to help save their client's life. When the lawyers talked about judges being fair, all they really meant was they knew there would be favoritism for the prosecution but as long as they could operate within the law then a judge was fair. This is a low bar that as the interviews make clear not every lawyer interviewed believed judges were able to hurdle. As to the prosecutors, it was exceptionally clear that overall the death penalty defense lawyers do not hold them in high regard personally or professionally.

With the ideological boundaries in place the death penalty defense lawyers, who are provided with 'adequate' resources, largely engage in an intense, aggressive and tenacious style of litigation practice that occurs first with a strong mitigation package to stop a case from ever going to trial then morphs into motions practice. The reality is that most of these cases are not 'who done it?' questions—the clients are usually, but not always, guilty. Nevertheless, if the mitigation package is strong enough, it can convince prosecutors to move off a death sentence and offer an LWOP plea. However, if a case is going to trial, then motions practice gives the lawyers a second chance to convince prosecutors to offer an LWOP plea or at least set the stage for a solid sentencing argument to the jury or in the case of a death sentence a very lengthy appeals processes.

In Colorado, even if a death penalty case is lost and the client is put on death row creating a strong enough trial record that can be used to litigate a massive amount of appellate issues might buy the client enough time for the law to change and convert the death sentence to LWOP. When Colorado had the 3-judge panel deciding death cases those who were sentenced to die by the judges had long enough appeals going so that when the panel was ruled unconstitutional all of those sentences were covered to LWOP. For the cases coming after the 3-judge panel was done away with the three death sentences of Sir Mario Owens, Nathan Dunlap and Rickey Reys were still in the appeals processes when then Governor John Hickenlooper put a moratorium on executions. This moratorium lasted up to the now Governor Jared Polis' term when he eventually signed the bill to end capital punishment in Colorado and converted all outstanding death sentences to LWOP.

The intense, aggressive and tenacious litigation practice from start to finish spared the lives of numerous people facing a death sentence in Colorado and is likely why only one person had been executed in the state since the *Furhman* decision reinstating capital punishment in America.

6

Sacrifice Within a Culture of Resistance

Fighting battles, whether they be for a moral, political or legal cause will inevitably require some form of sacrifice. The form of sacrifice will certainly vary by the type of battles being fought—sometimes people will sacrifice their life, and other times it is wealth, reputation, time or health. This is by no means an inclusive list. In a 2010 interview, Lynn Coffin, a 68 year old criminal defense lawyer, stated that: "It's a big toll on people to have clients on death row…Even if they are nowhere near execution, they are very needy. Most have no family connections anymore, no money, no friends, so the lawyer becomes the source of everything.… Emotionally it is very taxing.[1]" Each of the death penalty defense lawyers I interviewed talked about the realities of doing their work and it was very clear sacrificing things such as time and health is a given if the work is going to be done correctly. These sacrifices demonstrate the depth of their moral commitment to fighting against the death penalty.

---

[1] Dolan, Maura (2010). Lack of Funding Builds Death Row Log Jam. November 27, 2010. http://articles.latimes.com/2010/nov/27/local/la-me-death-lawyers-20101201.

My goal in this chapter is simply to highlight the reality that being part of a legal culture of resistance will require a level of personal sacrifice. The participants in this study were willing to make sacrifices not just in order to save their clients life but hopefully bring an end to capital punishment. No matter how inspiring or aspirational any of the lawyer's stories might be, there is a cost to be paid if anyone reading this book wants to pursue death penalty defense work.

One of the more memorable responses I got when asking about the time and sacrifice death penalty defense work requires came from Peter Reynolds. Reynolds' interview touches on so many of the issues the death penalty defense lawyers felt with when in litigation such as (1) time commitment, (2) health problems from stress and (3) perhaps drinking a little more alcohol than normal.

> *Interviewer:* "How many hours were you putting in a week?"
> *Well, when I was working only on [death penalty cases], 70 easy. I mean I wasn't married, I didn't have kids, it's what I did. I did that and I drank. And I played, I had a couple of, I had a girlfriend during part of that time and then that blew out. Those were always complicated situations.*
> *Interviewer:* "So then how did all that, how was it affecting you?"
> *...Well, it fucks you up. I mean there's just no way around it...It's all encompassing. There really is this sense, at least this is the sense I had, if you fuck up one little thing this could be the difference. And you know I've always believed, you know, part of being a good trial lawyer, especially from our end. I mean a good trial lawyer if you're a prosecutor basically means taking all the ducks that are already sitting there and making sure they stay in order best you can. For us, you know, we have to scratch and claw for any hand-hold generally. And then take the ones that we have and magnify them, the best we can. And so, it can mean, it really can mean that one little fucking thing, one little thing, you know, one little, can be the thing that turns the worm, I mean it really can.*
> *Interviewer:* "So I mean how did it, did it get to you physically at all?
> *Well, as you can see I'm a pretty hefty guy to begin with. Yeah, yeah, my wife will tell you that it wore me down a lot...I don't know that I got like deathly sick but you're so tired. Just worn, worn, worn down. The cases are long, jury selection takes forever, it's just long, long, long and hard. I was smoking in those days and you know, the relief really was drinking as much as anything. Not like, certainly not during the day, but you know, at the end*

6 Sacrifice Within a Culture of Resistance

of the day to kind of cut loose a little bit. And it just goes on forever and it's always on your mind. I mean, trials do that anyway…but [death penalty cases] were more.

Tina Carter similarly told me about the long hours, sacrifices in her personal life and a little more drinking than normal in large part due to the stress of these cases—which in one instance went on for three years.

Oh god, death penalty cases are so different…there's so much more detail in how you do it, it's just a different way. I couldn't even begin to tell you how many hours…it's just hours and hours and hours and hours of inputting so that you have this story to tell. Back in those days I wasn't married, seventy hour work weeks, eighty hours weren't uncommon.
Interviewer: "Did it ever affect you?"
I didn't get married until I was 48, so probably yeah, yeah.
Interviewer: "You don't have to go into this part if you don't want but with others, they have said there has been physical issues that have popped up because of all the time they're putting in and the stress."
I can tell you that when we got to trial on [REDACTED] I had bronchitis and I could not get rid of it through the entire trial. My co-counsel came down with pneumonia while we were waiting for the verdict and what happened with that case it misfired. And then we ended up pleading them to life. While we were waiting for the verdict, w were in a, because we had to try the case, we had to change the venue so we tried it in [REDACTED], and so we were living in a hotel. And we, I think it was two or three days we were waiting for the verdict, we never got out of the bed. We were so sick. So yes, it takes a physical toll on you. I had been on anti-depresents since [REDACTED] and I've never gone for of them, so sucre, there's physical and psychological difficulties that go with it.

Working a lot of hours and putting in long days was a very common theme among the lawyers I interviewed. Darrell Kappers gave me insight into what those long hours look like when in the middle of defending a death penalty case.

Interviewer: "How many hours were you putting in?"
It was just…constant; around the clock. We couldn't even keep up with what was coming in; you know there was just so much stuff coming in every

> day and one could have had a full time job just reading what was coming in but we were doing so much other stuff; we were doing mitigation by flying to [REDACTED], talking to family members and had a video crew come with us and we video tapped all the interviews with people and introduced those at the sentencing part of the trial, so we were doing all that and then mental health stuff, trial stuff, motions litigation stuff at the same time and we were in hearings for motions for like 3 weeks straight every other month and then 6-7 weeks off of court and then back for another 3 weeks and that went on for 2 years prior to trial and the trial itself lasted a long time. 5 weeks of jury selection and 16 weeks of trial.

In the last chapter, I discussed that a major component of defending death penalty cases is to engage in vigorous litigation by fighting every piece of evidence when reasonably possible. As such, working so many hours is not much of a surprise. However, the reality is that such a grueling trial schedule has its personal costs. A bit later in her interview, while discussing the stress of litigation, Tina Carter told me about the trouble she has sleeping while in trial.

> I have problems sleeping when I'm in trial, I have problems sleeping when I am upset about an outcome and a problem sleeping when I drink too much wine. It puts me right to bed and then I wake up.

Not sleeping well was also an issue for Clarice Montez while she was in trial.

> I don't sleep very well.
> Interviewer: "Why's that?"
> It's the stress. You know, I've talked with Charles Park about this many times actually, that waking up at 2 o'clock the morning thinking, 'Oh my god did I file that motion?' 'Oh my god, I should have argued that, I should have said this.' Really the concept that if I make a mistake, which I know I do every time I go into court, every day I'm going to make a mistake, every day I'm going to miss memorializing something and any mistake that I make could result in my client being killed. That's why I take melatonin and various other things, trust me, I've got a whole regiment. I make sure before bed to take my melatonin. You know, I don't think, I don't think many death penalty lawyers sleep well.

6 Sacrifice Within a Culture of Resistance

In the prior chapter, Brenda Telles talked about having over forty full days of motions hearings alone in one of her death penalty cases. Later in the interview, Brenda told me about the personal and physical sacrifices that come with the schedule and having to litigate cases that are often far away from home.

So I lived in a little apartment in [REDACTED] with milk crates, it was like being back in college. And the trial was in [REDACTED] so I'm away from my family and you know we picked the jury for seven weeks and you know, picking a jury for one day is stressful, picking a jury for seven weeks is just inhumane and ridiculous and unhealthy. So like the rush of adrenaline every single solitary day for that period of time, I don't know how we're not more sick than we are, I really don't. So stomach medications, illnesses, I've had shingles which if you Google it, say stress lowers your immunity, if your immunity's compromised then things like shingles show up. Almost like adult set asthma because I kept getting sick and I would cough and I couldn't stop coughing and I was doing like inhalers and steroids and stuff and this is all during that case that I went to trial on for twelve weeks. And since then it has let up; I've gotten better…But I think when you go to trial on a capital case you can guarantee physical stuff will occur. And my co-counsel ended up in the hospital, he thought he was having a heart attack and it was an ulcer. So I mean, it's not, it's everyone I know, they, everyone has their war stories of who went to the hospital during trial because someone always goes to the hospital during trial. You just, your body cannot, the moment you wake up it's like someone just flushes adrenaline into your stomach and it stays there. It's just awful.

Wyatt Desmond told me about his health problems but also informed me about issues other death penalty defense lawyers had who, at the time of the interview, had passed away:

During [REDACTED] I lost 17 pounds. I had constant stomach problems. I don't know any, I think death penalty lawyers either become obsessive with exercise or make themselves physically sick. After I got out of [REDACTED] I had to go, I went to a chiropractor for three solid months just to get my body straightened out. Because it's not, it's just there's no, you never can relax. You live and die on every word. I, by the end of that case I could barely stand up. My neck and back were in such bad shape. William Duggen had his guts scoped half dozen times, he has the worst reflux I've ever seen, you know? Some turn to drugs and alcohol. I suspect that's what killed [REDACTED]. It's a terrible, emotional and physical toll. I don't know anyone, we've had, you know there have been lawyers that we have passed the lore on to who have tried one case and quit. Not knowing, I'm hiring these, you know people come in and say, ultimately my goal is that I want to do death cases. It's like, no you don't, trust me, you don't want to do death cases. But it's like a drug in some ways. You get into these things and the stakes are so high, the adrenalines so high, the litigation level is the highest you will ever be. If I left this job, I don't know, I can't imagine going back and trying DUI cases. It would be difficult. Not because I think people that have DUIs are any less important, it's just a different level of juice. That make sense?

William Duggan discussed the health issue she experienced when defending death penalty cases where he worked "every waking hour."

Interviewer: "So as far as stress level goes, it seems pretty high."
Extremely high. Devastating. Body falls apart, it's hell. You know, there's damage. Physical as well as emotional damage ok?
Interviewer: "Do you mind going into any of that?"
I mean you don't form relationships with women very well because you're gone all the time. It's hard to tell, 'Where are you going?' 'Well this guy murdered everybody in the parking lot here so I gotta go down there and spend a year and a half down there, I'll be gone every day.' And you know, I'll be really cranky and upset. Sort of explosive, you know and I'll probably drink a little too much when I'm down there. And you know, then I'll have constricted esophagus from my acid reflux and I'll have you know, my skin will fall off. I'll have nervous situations. Then you kind of get a little PTSD'ed often, you know? I mean, you know, then you're down and then you're off a case and then boom another one comes back up, I mean, you know, it just, it was just…I mean then you start getting nervous you don't have one. Might as well get one because the next one's gonna be even worse, right? You know, that's what happens to you. I mean it's tough on you.

Duggan was not the only person to have stress even after a trial was over. Brenda Telles told me about still having memories of a death penalty trial well after it was concluded.

6 Sacrifice Within a Culture of Resistance

> *Well, even after the trial was over, I was dreaming about the trial and I remember sitting up in bed and saying 'it's over, I mean it's over, you won, it's over, you can sleep now.' I mean, so even after it's over and the threat is removed my mind was still obsessing and I just had a client who had PTSD so I studied a lot about PTSD and you know on a much smaller scale, the intrusive thoughts, the lack of sleep, you know, waking up in a cold sweat, many of the things associated with PTSD, obviously I'm not trying to say it's that, I wouldn't compare it to someone in combat, but certainly on a much lesser scale I certainly have intrusive thoughts, nightmares, trouble sleeping, anger, agitation, all the things they list I certain feel that I had just because of that one case.*

Larry Dunn also talked about how the massive amounts of hours put into a case take a physical toll on him when doing death penalty defense litigation.

> *Interviewer: "Time commitment wise what were you normally looking at?"*
>
> *Well, you're looking at the possibility of months long trial, anywhere from one month to two full months in trial, you're looking at dozens of hearing days and you're looking at huge amounts of investigation. I don't know what the total amount of hours put into a death penalty litigation is but it consumes you, it consumes your practice.*
>
> *Interviewer: "How does that affect friendships and the like?"*
>
> *Well, I mean if you're a death penalty defense lawyer you're hanging out with people who understand. It is not like my friends are all pissed off because they are like, 'hey man what is with all this death penalty bullshit?' They know, they get it. There are other things in the personal life though. I mean I am single and frequently unavailable when I am involved in this stuff and for some people, well I just want someone who is more available. Physically it breaks you down that is for sure, the skin on my fingertips peel a little bit, had an early ulcer and well, I just knew the stress was getting to me during these cases. Tired all the time but it is what it is.*

Lewis Frankfurter told me more about how the time commitment can have adverse effects on a private practice and a lawyer's family.

> You can maintain several other cases but the death penalty litigation takes up 75% of your time…As you get close to trial, usually working sixty, seventy hours a week.
>
> Interviewer: "We're going to get into a little more personal stuff with this so if you don't want to answer that's perfectly OK. But I mean, how did that affect you personally? Having spent so much time working on these cases. How did it affect your life outside of work?"
>
> You lose money. And if you're married and have kids it's hard on them because you're never home. So some tension develops there. You turn away clients and other cases you would like to do, but you just can't because of the commitment. So it's, there's a business impact and there's a personal and family impact. Depending on how you handle it, the stress of it can physically affect you. Depending on how you handle it.
>
> Interviewer: "Did that happen to you? Any physical?"
>
> Yeah, I'm sure it did. The scary thing about that is that a lot of it is probably beneath the surface and subtle and intangible and insidious and you don't even realize it at the time.

Of all the lawyers I interviewed, only Rita Townsend was willing to talk about the time period before witnessing an execution—granted she was one of only a few that actually had to see one—and the feelings associated with trying so hard to save a client's life and not succeeding.

> …for me last year leading up to um, [REDACTED]'s execution was actually worse for me because I felt really helpless. During the [REDACTED] clemency I felt like, I felt like we were accomplishing something, I mean, it was a ton of work and there's no let up and we couldn't stop and I was scared because I can feel the positive momentum but I felt like it could go south for us at any moment. But I really felt like we were getting somewhere and I was very hopeful. I did not feel that way in the time leading up to [REDACTED]'s execution and both during the briefing of that case and then you know sometime later when we were leading up to the execution, I just felt really scared and hopeless and that. I was having trouble sleeping and just, you know, feeling a lot of physical effects of stress. My way of dealing with that is mostly to get exercise and to talk about it. I think you have to let yourself feel what you're feeling. If you try to bottle it up and hide it it's gonna hurt you.

Finally, two of the lawyers didn't want to talk about the problems they faced during litigation. Uniquely, only Carl Reese and Christopher Nelson told me that they really did not have any trouble with sleeping, relational or physical problems and the like. For instance, here is what Carl Reese told me in his interview about the lack of problems so many other defense lawyers felt:

> *It's the compartmentalizing. It's not good, but I didn't notice any particular, I mean clearly you have an increased stress level and everything else but I wouldn't say I noticed it. I mean I probably didn't sleep as well but it wasn't to the point of becoming problematic.*

Conclusion

Overall, the death penalty defense attorneys by and large know that this type of work is incredibly harmful for their health and well-being but they keep on taking cases. Their personal anger towards the death penalty and belief that nobody should ever be executed by the government not only helps keep the lawyers motivated to do this work but willing to accept physical, mental and financial harm. Without the willingness to sacrifice, a culture of resistance is not likely to be created or sustained. As such, the willingness to sacrifice is a necessary component in a culture of resistance.

7

Conclusion

Nobody can say with any certainty that the death penalty in Colorado would not have been abolished without the work done by the lawyers interviewed in this monograph. Even before abolition, Colorado's death penalty apparatus was seen as largely symbolic.[1] Prior to abolition then Governor John Hickenlooper said the following when staying the execution of Nathan Dunlap: "If the State of Colorado is going to undertake the responsibility of executing a human being, the system must operate flawlessly. Colorado's system for capital punishment is not flawless."[2] In the context of this book, Hickenlooper's statement is very telling, but as demonstrated time and again, hardly unique.[3]

As I argue in these pages, the Colorado death penalty defense lawyers created a culture of resistance. This culture led to their many successes in

---

[1] Kaufman, Sarah Beth (2020). *American Roulette. The Social Logic of Death Penalty Sentencing Trials*. California University Press: Berkley, CA.

[2] Ray, Kelsey (2015). *Does Colorado's Death Penalty have a Race Problem?* The Colorado Independent. https://www.coloradoindependent.com/2015/08/20/does-colorados-death-penalty-have-a-race-problem/. August 20, 2015.

[3] Baumgartner, Frank, Marty Davidsion, Kanesha R. Johnson, Arvind Krishmuthy and Colin P. Wilson (2017). *Deadly Justice. A Statistical Portrait of the Death Penalty*. Oxford University Press: New York.

securing life sentences for their clients whether the decision makers were judges or juries. In fact, one could argue that Colorado's capital punishment apparatus was an 'ideal type' when thinking about just how difficult it was to secure a death sentence in the state and all the factors that go into getting an LWOP outcome. Even then, this monograph does expose serious flaws with even a well-structured capital punishment apparatus—assuming the perceptions of the death penalty defense lawyers are largely accurate—such as the reality that capital punishment in Colorado and around the country is more or less sought for political considerations of government bureaucrats as opposed to 'seeking justice[4]'—a reality consistent with Hickenlooper's critiques.

Whether the death penalty should exist as a method of punishment is a social, moral and political issue that goes beyond the scope of this monograph. Readers can and should educate themselves about the realities of capital punishment in America when deciding if the ultimate punishment is worthy of continuation. That said, so long as the death penalty is around defendants facing a possible execution will need the absolute best representation from attorneys.

Antonin Scalia argued in a dissent that the Constitution does not forbid the execution of an innocent person so long as they had a 'full and fair' trial.[5] This dissent is from a habeas corpus petition where a man named Troy Anthony Davis, who was put on death row for the killing of a law enforcement officer, requested a new trial because seven key witness' recanted their trial testimony and several individuals implicated the government's principal witness as the actual shooter of the deceased law enforcement officer.[6] In other words, for Scalia and other justices in agreement with him, evidence of actual innocence for a murder that was not available during the original trial is no reason to halt an execution based upon the Constitution so long as the original trial can be

---

[4] Gordon and Huber (2009). "The Political Economy of Prosecution." *Annual Review of Law and Social Science*, 5(1): 135–156; Bright and Keenan (1995). "Judges and the Politics of Death: Deciding Between the Bill of Rights and the Next Election in Capital Cases." *Boston University Law Review*, 73(2): 759–848; Levine and Cooke (2015). In States with Elected High Court Judges, a Harder Line on Capital Punishment. *Reuters*, Sept. 22, 2015.

[5] *In Re Davis*, 577 U.S. ____ (2009). (Scalia, A., dissenting).

[6] Id at 2.

interpreted as full and fair. What is considered a 'full and fair' trial is essentially in the eyes of the beholder. Prior to his expressed doctrinal position about newly discovered evidence of innocence, Scalia wrote the following about a man named Henry Lee McCollum when arguing in favor of the death penalty:

> ...for example, the case of the 11-year-old girl raped by four men and then killed by stuffing her panties down her throat. See McCollum v. North Carolina, cert. pending, No. 93-7200. How enviable a quiet death by lethal injection compared with that![7]

20 years later Justice Breyer would point out in a dissent arguing against the constitutionality of the death penalty that Henry Lee McCollum was exonerated by DNA evidence.[8] Scalia did not seem to care. In that same dissent Justice Breyer pointed out that we have credible evidence that innocent people have been put to death.[9] In fact, Breyer specifically mentions that former Colorado governor Bill Ritter granted a full and unconditional posthumous pardon to Joe Arridy, a man who was executed in 1936 possessing an IQ of 46 despite an overwhelming body of evidence indicating the 23-year-old Arridy was innocent, including false and coerced confessions, the likelihood that Arridy was not in Pueblo, CO at the time of the killing and an admission of guilt by someone else existed.[10]

Justice Blackmun wrote in a decent the following about what the ideal type of death penalty litigation should look like just before the execution of Bruce Callins:

> Within days, or perhaps hours, the memory of Callins will begin to fade. The wheels of justice will churn again, and somewhere, another jury or another judge will have the unenviable task of determining whether some human being is to live or die. We hope, of course, that the defendant whose life is at risk will be represented by competent counsel — someone

---

[7] *Callins v. Collins*, 510 U.S. 1141, 1143 (1994).
[8] *Glossip v. Gross*, 576 U.S. 863, 935-36 (2015) (Breyer, S. dissenting).
[9] Id.
[10] Id at 910-11.

who is inspired by the awareness that a less than vigorous defense truly could have fatal consequences for the defendant. We hope that the attorney will investigate all aspects of the case, follow all evidentiary and procedural rules, and appear before a judge who is still committed to the protection of defendants' rights — even now, as the prospect of meaningful judicial oversight has diminished. In the same vein, we hope that the prosecution, in urging the penalty of death, will have exercised its discretion wisely, free from bias, prejudice, or political motive, and will be humbled, rather than emboldened, by the awesome authority conferred by the State.[11]

The ideal type of process Blackmun describes simply does not exist—we know prosecutors hide or fabricate evidence to secure convictions and the courts have made it clear the wrongly convicted cannot seek civil monetary damages in these instances despite such serious injustice.[12] We also know there are judges like Scalia that are almost giddy when to comes to executing human beings deemed despicable enough which gives reason to think some judges are simply too biased to be fair arbiters. Given these realities, the only person standing in the way of a wrongful conviction ending in the execution of an innocent or people being put to death who do not deserve it are defense lawyers. Active resistance to the prosecutorial quest for an execution within a judicial system that contains judges willing to execute innocent people so long as they deem a trial to be full and fair no matter what new evidence arises in the future needs to be a cultural norm in order to give life to the ideal defense lawyer envisioned by Justice Blackmun.

It is my belief that to have the best death penalty defense lawyers available, there needs to be a cadre of attorneys that can create and sustain a culture of resistance. Courts continually engaged in what Justice Harry Blackmun called the experiment of constitutional regulation[13] in order to ensure the death penalty was fairly and constitutionally

---

[11] *Callins*, 510 U.S. 1141 at 1143 (Blackmun, J. dissenting).
[12] See generally, *Imbler v. Pachtman*, 424 U.S. 409 (1976); *Buckley v. Fitzsimmons*, 509 U.S. 259 (1993); *Connick v. Thompson*, 563 U.S. 51 (2011).
[13] *Callins v. Collins*, 510 U.S. 1141, 1145 (1994) (Blackmun, J., dissenting from denial of certiorari).

administered—an experiment that in many ways was a failure.[14] Thus, it seems that the only real protections anyone can count on when it comes to ensuring capital punishment is fairly administered rests upon the shoulders of death penalty defense lawyers.

Theoretically speaking, this book makes a simple argument: A culture of resistance is most likely to be created and sustained when a majority of death penalty defense attorneys are (1) from a young age socialized in a manner that encourages skepticism of government narratives and policies, (2) which later manifests into behaviors of non-conformity and active protest in college, (3) have meaningful experiences that are essentially life shaping in their internship or clinical programs during law school, (4) fully embrace the adversarial approach to litigation and are willing to at least accept, if not fully believe, judges and prosecutors are partisan adversaries in favor of capital punishment thus creating ideological boundaries, (5) are willing to fight aggressively and tenaciously on behalf of their clients in death penalty cases and (6) accept the sacrifices that come with being a capital defender. Furthermore, the lawyers need to be working within a legal arena that provides (a) adequate funding and (b) enough leniency to let the lawyers aggressively and fully litigate their cases. If the death penalty is to exist, then governments and criminal defense organizations need to create an environment where a culture of resistance can be formed and sustained.

Creating a theoretical framework focusing on the culture of death penalty defense lawyers and understanding how it likely helped bring about abolition of capital punishment is important but hardly provides a complete understanding as to why the attorneys were so successful and abolition finally did arrive. Colorado appears to be unique in what the defense lawyers have been able to accomplish. Whether or not other capital defense attorneys across the country have created a culture of resistance is an open question. As Garrett, Jakubow and Desai note, there is, nationally speaking, a serious decline over the last few years in the use and pursuit of capital punishment with less than 1% of counties in the

---

[14] See generally Steiker, Carol S. and Jordan M. Steiker (2016). *Courting Death. The Supreme Court and Capital Punishment*. The Belknap Press of Harvard University Press: Cambridge, MA.

country seeking the death penalty.[15] Colorado mirrors these trends as I stated in the introduction and there is simply no denying the death penalty defense lawyers play a role in this decline. However, it is unclear how large a role the attorneys play. Looking at the lawyers is only one piece in a much larger picture. Future studies should try to situate their findings in broader cultural processes—admittedly I did not go down such a path in this book. Changing population demographics, homicide rates, shifts in cultural sentiments about punishment and the like can, and probably do, play a role in explaining why the death penalty is used far less frequently than in the past and is being abolished in more states every year. Even the lawyers seem to understand they are just one part of a larger picture. Charles Park told me when I interviewed him after abolition that he felt their work was necessary because it allowed for *"...society to catch up with us."* Park's statement echoes Michael Meltsner, a prominent death penalty defense lawyer working for the famed Legal Defense Fund, who said *"The politics of abolition boiled down to this: for each year the United States went without executions, the more hollow would ring claims that the American people could not do without them.*[16]*"* While they may only be part of a larger picture the death penalty defense lawyers are still essential when it comes not just to winning LWOP cases but bringing about the abolition of capital punishment.

Admittedly, this monograph was not written for the purposes of informing public policy or advocating in any way, shape or form in regard to the death penalty. Nevertheless, there are some public policy implications worthy of brief discussion. A disturbing truth about criminal defense work as a whole is that public and private lawyers are woefully underfunded and understaffed in comparison to the resources prosecutors are provided by local, state and federal governments. Most criminal defendants simply cannot afford to hire expert witnesses, fund separate investigations, and with lawyers being overworked cases simply do not get the attention they need to be fully litigated. What Colorado

---

[15] Garrett, Brandon, Alexander Jakubow and Ankur Desai (2017). "The American Death Penalty Decline." *The Journal of Criminal Law & Criminolgoy*, 107(4): 561–642.

[16] Meltsner, Michael (1973). *Cruel and Unusual: The Supreme Court and Capital Punishment*. Random House Publishing: New York.

showed is that when defense lawyers are given 'adequate resources' and the playing field becomes more level outcomes favoring prosecutors at any stage, especially sentencing, are far from certain even in a system seemingly stacked completely against criminal defendants. As such, the outcomes of prosecutions are more likely to be seen as fair and equitable when defenders are provided 'adequate resources.' At a time when the confidence in America's criminal processing system is low, providing greater funds to public and private criminal defense lawyers so the playing field is more equitable with prosecutors needs to be at the very least considered. I can say from personal experience that when I was on even footing with prosecutors during any stage of litigation my outcomes at trial and sentencing were far more advantageous for clients.

Ironically though, an effective culture of resistance whether it be in the death penalty context or otherwise might be a reason to keep certain punitive practices in place. Practicing death penalty defense attorneys around the country have asked themselves if in the end, they are "serving to legitimate the system by helping to provide sanitized executions, executions with the aura of legalism and therefore the appearance of fairness."[17] Specific to the death penalty, each one of the lawyers I interviewed demonstrated what is possible when highly skilled attorneys with adequate funding can do even while working in a system they all generally saw as unfair and biased against criminal defendants. However, winning multiple LWOP sentences may be all proponents of capital punishment need to claim that the system as a whole is in fact operating legally, constitutionally and fairly despite significant evidence of arbitrary application and racial discrimination within the death penalty apparatus.

All that aside, my hope with this monograph is to demonstrate that the Colorado death penalty defense lawyers, as a collective, created a culture of resistance which helped bring about abolition of capital punishment in the state. What lessons can be learned from this book and reasonably implemented are up to those doing criminal defense work. Most importantly though, I wanted to tell the stories of some of the

---

[17] Michael Mello, Another Attorney for Life, in Facing the Death Penalty: Essays on a Cruel and Unusual Punishment 87 (Michael L. Radelet ed., 1989).

most amazingly dedicated and skilled attorneys I have ever met—they resemble everything a criminal defense lawyer should be—they represent everything we as citizens should expect out of criminal defense lawyers if our Constitution's guarantee of competent counsel is to mean anything. I hope I told their stories well.

Epilog

Unfortunately, I was not able to catch up with all the attorneys for follow-up interviews after abolition. I was able to get in contact with Charles Park, Clarice Montez, Brenda Telles and Tina Carter. Clarice Montez was the only one still actively practicing with a full client list, Tina Carter only had one case that had just wrapped up and her plan was to retire. Brenda Telles and Charles Park retired almost immediately after abolition.

Of those I was not able to speak with after abolition, I learned Carl Reese, Peter Reynolds, Ricky Davis, William Duggan and Lewis Frankfurter have retired, Wyatt Desmond is still practicing as a public defender but in a much smaller capacity. Charles Nelson is a solo practitioner still doing criminal defense work. Rita Townsend and Larry Dunn are the only lawyers actively taking death penalty cases in the trial or appellate phase, but their work is in federal court or out of state.

In speaking with Charles Park, Clarice Montez, Brenda Telles and Tina Carter, they were all incredibly happy about the death penalty being repealed in Colorado. Charles Park told me he had been saving a bottle of champagne for over 15 years specifically for abolition and drank it that very evening with his wife. Clarice Montez told me that at the news of abolition, she was "*overwhelmed with joy and I had kinda collapsed* with the emotion…its too bad that it happened over COVID because we would have had one wild fucking party like you wouldn't believe!" When I told Brenda Telles about Clarice's thoughts on a party, she laughed heartedly and said "*yeah, I would've attended!*" That said, Brenda told me she simply felt relief and that it was such an 'emotional dump' that she wasn't sure exactly how to feel—she could only describe her feeling as relief. Tina also talked about how happy she was but admitted feeling a bit guilty for lawyers in other states where capital punishment will likely never go away such as Mississippi, Texas and Georgia. Tina told me she felt guilty because "*I know what those lawyers are going through – what they are feeling, and my joy is tempered by that fact it [the death penalty]is still there.*"

I also asked them about how they saw their role in abolition. All four told me they had generally just focused on the case in front of them and worked to save their clients life—securing life sentences as a means to the abolition of capital punishment was never an immediate goal…it was a hope. Nevertheless, as Charles Park put it, abolition "*was a collective effort. Winning these cases set the stage to make it easier to argue it is a useless appendage to the criminal justice system.*"

One thing I was interested in now that abolition occurred was to know if it meant somehow murder cases would be much less likely to plea out as was a concern of prosecutors like George Brauchler. During the follow-up interview, Clarice Montez told me that she hardly ever had murder cases dealt out before abolition and in current cases, they still go to trial because prosecutors always ask for 1st degree murder even in cases that, as she put it, 'should deal.' Clarice told me that "*Often times, DAs won't even make us an offer so we have to go to trial anyway.*" Her point is simpe—the behavior of district attorneys in homicide litigation did not change even with abolition. Benda Telles, Tina Carter and Charles Park agreed with these sentiments.

Despite their joy, there remains a concern that the death penalty can still come back. During the follow-up interviews, there was a mass shooting at a King Soopers in Boulder, CO and for a brief moment, talk of bringing back the death penalty emerged. I asked Brenda Telles about this and she felt that even if the case was tried as a capital case, the outcome is already known: LWOP. For the time being, Colorado's experiment with capital punishment seems to be at an end and it is in no small part to the commitment and sacrifices made by the state's death penalty defense lawyers. If there is any justice in this world, the next generation of criminal defense lawyers will learn how to defend all criminal cases like the attorneys I interviewed—it seems to be the only way to give life to the Constitution's guarantee of having competent counsel. As Charles Park put it in the final interview: "*It is up to the new generation of defense lawyers to ensure the death penalty doesn't come back.*"

No matter what happens, knowing everything I now know about what these lawyers went through and accomplished in their careers, I have my own hope—that they all live the rest of their lives in joy and peace.

GPSR Compliance

The European Union's (EU) General Product Safety Regulation (GPSR) is a set of rules that requires consumer products to be safe and our obligations to ensure this.

If you have any concerns about our products, you can contact us on

ProductSafety@springernature.com

In case Publisher is established outside the EU, the EU authorized representative is:

Springer Nature Customer Service Center GmbH
Europaplatz 3
69115 Heidelberg, Germany

www.ingramcontent.com/pod-product-compliance
Lightning Source LLC
LaVergne TN
LVHW020348260326
834688LV00045B/1592